A SANDHILLS READER:
Thirty Years of Great Writing from the Great Plains

A SANDHILLS READER:

Thirty Years of Great Writing from the Great Plains

Edited by

Mark Sanders

Stephen F. Austin State University Press

Nacogdoches, Texas

For more information:
Stephen F. Austin State University Press
P.O. Box 13007 SFA Station
Nacogdoches, Texas 75962
sfapress@sfasu.edu
www.sfasu.edu/sfapress

Distributed by Texas A&M Consortium
www.tamupress.com

LIBRARY OF CONGRESS CATALOGING-IN-PUBLICATION
DATA

Sanders, Mark
A Sandhills Reader. Thirty Years of Great Writing from the Great
Plains / Mark Sanders

p.cm.
ISBN: 978-1-62288-150-5

ACKNOWLEDGMENTS ℰꝋ

Gracious appreciation to the publishers for permission to reprint the following work:

Barton Sutter, "Swedish Lesson," "Geneva," "Halloween on Hennepin," and "Shoe Shop" from *The Book of Names: New and Selected Poems*. Originally collected in *Pine Creek Parish Hall and Other Poems*. Copyright © 1985, 1993 by Barton Sutter. Reprinted with the permission of the author and BOA Editions, Ltd., www.boaeditions.org.

"The Poem," originally printed as a Main-Traveled Roads chapbook, is being reprinted by permission from *History, Passion, Freedom, Death, and Hope: Prose about Poetry* by Kelly Cherry (Tampa: University of Tampa Press, 2005).

All other selections were provided for reprint by the author. We appreciate their continued generosity toward the editor and toward both the Stephen F. Austin State University Press and Sandhills Press.

Much appreciation to Kirstie Linstrom and Kimberly Verhines of SFA Press for rescuing this work and for designing the book. Thanks to Tinesha Mix for making the last set of corrections.

Special acknowledgment to Corinne Jones, who so graciously permitted me the use of her Sandhill Crane that grace this cover.

This book is dedicated to Kimberly, pressing onward.

TABLE OF CONTENTS

ℰℭ

&

INTRODUCTION ❧

Something possessed me. In 1978, had I been more experienced, I might never have started a small press. I am certain Sandhills Press came into existence for all the wrong reasons, among them youthful stubbornness and an arrogance I have long since traded away.

Sandhills started as a reaction against editors of other journals, other presses. I had determined, as early as 1975, that I wanted to write poetry and fiction; I imagined I would be immediately successful—what young writer does not hold such delusions? But, my earliest attempts at writing and publishing were not successful. Far from it. The first batches of poetry I submitted all returned to me, all standard rejection forms save one, which read: "You need more practice anyway."

Thus, I endeavored to practice and did not submit my work for nearly two years, in part to get better, in part to avoid the harsh criticism. I took a creative writing course at Kearney State College (now the University of Nebraska at Kearney) with Don Welch, who would become my mentor for the next several years. At his encouragement (not his urging), because I had written some reasonably successful pieces, I submitted work to the college's *Platte Valley Review,* two journals from Texas, and one more from outstate Nebraska, and had poems accepted by all the editors except the one at my college, the editor who knew me as a disinterested student. We had a conversation. He told me the writing was substandard and discouraged me from continuing to write.

Such was the less than impressive beginning of my writing career, but Dr. Grundy's insistence that I should not write poetry was also the impetus that convinced me to begin Sandhills Press. I was sure he did not know what he was talking about, and, having pitched the press idea to Ted Kooser, William Kloefkorn, and Don Welch, all of them receptive to the notion, I commenced editorship, to show him I had more mettle for the task than he himself did. I purposely told Dr. Grundy that I was starting a press. I knew it would provoke. We argued; he claimed I was encroaching upon his territory. I affirmed there was enough poetry to go around. As I said, I was arrogant. My motives had been less than wholly honorable.

Early in 1979, I published the first of Sandhills' books, a chapbook of poetry I had authored, entitled *First Hunt,* just as a trial. I will not lay any claims regarding the quality of the poetry, but the publication roused the attentions of a number of folks, including Dr. Grundy, who graciously noted that, while he had tried to discourage me from the enterprise, he thought what I had done and could do would be of value. It was the first of a number of positive responses that goaded me toward continuing the press and its attention to Great Plains writers. The press's first anthology, *The Sandhills & Other Geographies: An Anthology of Nebraska Poetry,* appeared in 1980; it was my regional response to Edward Field's *A Geography of Poets* and Lucien Stryk's the *Heartland* anthologies published several years before. I remember remarking to friends that my goal was to publish as author or editor one book every two years. I find, all these years later, that I exceeded the mark. I quit counting about five years into the effort.

I have taken the Sandhills with me wherever I have lived—the press and its Nebraska presence have accompanied me to regions remote and dissimilar from the region that I knew intimately. And all the while I published, on the shoe-string and rarely with any grant assistance. When the Nebraska Center for the Book awarded me the Mildred Bennett Award in 2007 for "fostering Nebraska's literary heritage," due to my writing about Nebraska, writing about Nebraska's writers, and publishing Nebraska writers, I had not really considered that I had been at the helm of a small press for so many years. As I told the audience at the awards dinner, I truly did not have any clear idea about how many books, chapbooks, or broadsides I had published; I have tried to make a comprehensive listing of the works, but I know I am missing some of the titles. I have actually given away many of my own personal copies, and virtually everything that Sandhills has done over the years quickly went out of print. While the Bennett Award was a big honor for me, I was not sure I deserved the recognition which, by the way, placed me in the company of my earliest mentors and supporters: Kloefkorn, Kooser, and Welch.

I have threatened to stop Sandhills Press often; and, for every threat, there has been a book in response. Still the reactionary, still stubborn, I realize now, past my early arrogance, that presswork is about as selfless a thing that I have ever done. I have not made loads of money doing Sandhills Press books; at most, I sometimes receive appreciation from the authors whose work I have brought to print—sometimes not. It has been a solitary activity, and, often, I have done it at the expense of my own writing. Even so, giving Sandhills Press thirty years of my life has also been among the pleasurable times. I understand that small presses rarely last as long as this press has. Perhaps this is a miracle. More miraculous is the writing the reader will find in these pages.

Although this book was projected for publication in 2009, delays and circumstances postponed its arrival. Indeed, all the authors' prefaces were written in 2009. Thus, I apologize to the writers whose work is included here and who had looked for an earlier delivery date. Sandhills books have always been subjected to varieties of trial, so this collection stands in good company. As an explanatory note, Sandhills has had a number of imprints, notably Talking River Publications and Lewis-Clark Press, the latter helmed by my wife, Kimberly Verhines. I debated long about including work in this anthology from those books but ultimately decided against it, though, if I were to put an estimate on the quantity of books published by Talking River and LC Press, there are an additional three-dozen titles—many of them no longer in our possession. Our mission was to get new literature out, but we were not always careful archivists as, in principle, collecting often has little to do with creating.

I cannot anticipate at this time whether Sandhills will continue in any active capacity—I feel deep need these days to write. I plan on doing another anthology devoted to friends and friends of Sandhills Press—a sort of literary reunion—and I recently continued my effort in behalf of words by joining Stephen Meats at *The Midwest Quarterly* in co-editing *Three Generations of Nebraska Poets* (52.4, 2011). As for Kimberly, she and Stephen F. Austin State University began SFA Press on that campus in 2009; I am not directly involved, though I have made recommendations for Plains writers whose work must not be overlooked. Thus, I am always the advocate for great writing from the Great Plains, but Kimberly is the strong arm and standard bearer for Nebraska and Great Plains writers now.

—Mark Sanders, Nacogdoches, Texas
August 2015

DAVID BAKER ℘

David Baker was born in Bangor, Maine, and has spent more than forty years of his life in the Midwest. He has authored seven volumes of poetry, including *Never-Ending Birds*, and he is the poetry editor for *The Kenyon Review*. An Ohio resident for over twenty years, he is a professor of English at Denison University where he holds the Thomas B. Fordham Chair of Creative Writing. The poems included here come from *Holding Katherine*, which Sandhills published in 1996 as part of the Main-Traveled Road Chapbook series.

NOTE FROM BAKER ABOUT SANDHILLS PRESS

It's hard to believe that Mark Sanders has been shepherding the Sandhills Press now for thirty years. That's real longevity, especially in today's literary scene, where Facebook poets tout their slender skills to each other and blog-verse vanishes into the electric ether as quickly as it appears. But after all, most of the trade presses are reducing or eliminating their poetry lists, and university presses must strain mightily to survive the threats of extinction, and sometimes lose. I salute Mark and am grateful for the contributions—to the region and reading public—of his press. Small presses can play a large role.

In 1996 Sandhills Press published *Holding Katherine*, a chapbook which Ann Townsend and I co-authored. Co-authoring was part of our experience as parents; after all, we co-authored a daughter, Katherine Girard Baker, in 1992. The chapbook is our album of delights and perils from those first few years. Some of those poems later ended up in full-length books of ours, respectively, and some of the poems are collected here and nowhere else.

This publication remains the one most dear to me, given its subject, its nature, and its co-authorship. Mark was immediately hospitable to the idea and, in fact, so gracious that he contributed his own pen-and-ink drawing, based on a number of the poems, to serve as cover art to *Holding Katherine*.

Katherine—Katie—is now seventeen. She is a high-school senior. Don't tell her I told you this: She keeps a copy of *Holding Katherine* on her bedside bookcase and sometimes shows her friends. Sometimes I find it open to one page, sometimes another. Nothing means more to me than that. I leave it as I find it, each time.

႘

CHILDLESS

They have found us sleeping during snow once again.
The great horned owls call out in white winds,
turning their hooded crowns over our night.
We must walk one hardened acre to the creek
to stand with them where they wait. How can we not?
They have brought back the cry we heard once
as a child's, far away, lost, and asking our name.

HOME

Again the time has come to take our morning walk.
Look beneath the heavy cedars, little dear.
Deer have stayed here overnight. Their hooves
have left some tell-tale moons and hearts in
innocent dry sands along our bending creek.
Creatures of many hungers say we're near.
Hear them call our human name. Like your mother,
her voice floating down the distant air
where we have come awhile, they sing us back
because they fear our straying out too far,
farther than the deep woods reach. Because we
went without her knowing we'd be gone, hear
her sweet voice cry above the others come back in.
In time we'll let it lead us home again.

HOLDING KATHERINE

Let us look up tonight where the white trees surround us.
Let us face once again the spinning stars going dim,
going cold, to stretch a while beside your one window.
Many blue arms reach down the cedars and oaks.
Like coins, brief insects glitter and toss in the glow
of streetlamps lining the lane where nobody goes for a time.
In the cradle of a new father's arms, can you hear them fall?
Once in a dream you swam in a blue dress dazzled with sun
through a garden of flowers toward me. I wrote your name
in my tablet when I woke, knowing it like the trace
of a habit handed hack from the blood, knowing your face
like my own and your arms as I held you for the first time.
The star chamber swirls overhead like oceans of white hair
sparked by the wind or the tentative call of night birds
spinning their place through the tremulous dark and breeze.
Trucks groan miles distant on the highway, heading away.
You have traveled so far to be here, farther than they have
and farther than I down the winding tunnel from when time
was a speck brilliant with nothing but hope for us or despair.
Soon we will sit back to rock a while longer through
the hungry night always within us. I will sing you your name.
I will surround you with bright eyes of toys and soft sheets.
I will go quiet like this night when I go, as the light
of far stars burns in your sky from a lifetime to come.

JIM BARNES ᔓ

Jim Barnes taught at Truman State University from 1970 to 2003, where he was Professor of Comparative Literature and Writer-in-Residence. After retiring from Truman State, he was Distinguished Professor of English and Creative Writing at Brigham Young University. Jim married Cora Barnes McKown, artist and designer, in 2006. They now make their home a few miles east of Atoka, Oklahoma, on the McKown family ranch, and in Santa Fe, New Mexico. Jim is the founding editor of the Chariton Review Press and of *The Chariton Review*. He has published over 500 poems in more than 100 journals, including *Poetry*, *The Sewanee Review*, *The Kenyon Review*, *The Nation*, *The Chicago Review*, *The American Scholar*, *Prairie Schooner*, and *The Georgia Review*. His newest book of poetry is *Visiting Picasso* (University of Illinois Press, 2007).

Sandhills published these two poems in the 1991 anthology, *The Decade Dance: A Celebration of Poems*.

ᔓ

THESE DAMNED TREES CROUCH

(for W. D. Snodgrass)

These damned trees crouch heavy under heaven.
As I crouch, if I talk, I often cuss
this confounded wood and my own soft heart.
Some hunters like this place and rise at seven
and stand in ease in weather like a lush;
Jim Barnes is crawling through the underbrush.

I don't know why I cannot find my house.
It ought to be around here somewhere. Fuss
and bother: the crooked tree, the skunk's art
lingering on till dark to then arouse

all sleeping demons of the mighty bush;
Jim Barnes is crawling through the underbrush.

My name is just as common as a worm,
and derivative. If I should converse just
with something inside myself and know it
(have a tete-a-tete with some small gentle germ),
I'd make a beeline home—that's where it starts.
Yes…most of all I'd like to be a poet.
But the wood is thick and won't allow old Herm
to come right winging down. I have to rush.

I have to find my house even though it hurts;
Jim Barnes is crawling through the underbrush.

TOUCHING THE RATTLESNAKE

The neighbor's leg was black from toe to thigh,
with yellow pus oozing from cuts he'd made
trying to stop the poison from reaching
his heart. He showed the three of us stumbling
into his house after Sunday school set
us free what he said we would be afraid
to see. The swollen blackness made me shudder
with adolescent sins I knew we were doomed
to hell for. He dared us to touch the leg.

Tight as the shell of a dried gourd, the skin
seemed to break with each slight movement he made.
I left with the smell of venom in my lungs,
my eyes careful with every rock we passed
on the way to the swimming hole. I lay
on the shoal and felt the current crawl along
my body until all thoughts of fangs were washed
away and the rattle of leaves above my head
seemed only leaves. *Amazing grace, how sweet*

I sang straight up into the Sunday sky.

The others splashed my face, and we wallowed
like carp in the mud. We could not know that one
of us would die before the sun went down, fangs
buried in his neck as he reached over a boulder
to pull himself up the face of the cliff above
the swimming hole. Nor that he would live just
long enough to climb back down, boasting that
he touched the snake before it struck his neck.

The neighbor did not die, but thrived on guts
he said it took to have a snaky leg.
I could not forget the oozying blackness
and never crossed his door again, nor how
white the naked body of my friend lay.
The wind rose late that day and made the limbs
crash above our heads. That night it rained.
The sound of thunder and shotguns carried us
through a domain of snakes we would annihilate.

STEPHEN C. BEHRENDT &

Poet Stephen C. Behrendt is George Holmes Distinguished Professor of English at the University of Nebraska-Lincoln, where he also serves as a reader and Contributing Editor for *Prairie Schooner*. His first collection of poems, *Instruments of the Bones* (1992) won the First Series Award from Mid-List Press. His most recent books of poetry are *History* (Mid-List Press, 2005) and *A Step in the Dark* (Mid-List Press, 1996). He is also the author of *Reading William Blake* (Macmillan) and many books of criticism, articles, and reviews.

The selections here come from *The PlainSense of Things 2: Eight Poets from Lincoln, Nebraska* (1997).

NOTE FROM BEHRENDT ABOUT SANDHILLS PRESS

Why Sandhills Press? Why any "small" or "regional" press? It's a good question, and one that flies in the face of the big commercial presses and the way they do their business. For them, it's just that—business. For smaller, more regionally based operations like Sandhills Press—and dozens and dozens of others one might name—it's not so much business as it is passion. I want to say " pleasure," rather than passion, but the two are inseparable in fact. Ask any of the publishers who wrestle with the hydra-headed issues of budget (first and last), clean copy, deadlines, good submissions and day-to-day editorial chores. Yes, it's a passion, surely, as Mark Sanders and other editors and publishers will quickly testify. But there is of course also that element of pleasure that drives everything, finally. Pleasure at finding good writing, new writing, lively stuff that is not just more of the mainstream, trendy material of the "big" publishers but is, rather, inflected with a more "local" voice and habitation. And publishing it, of course.

This sort of writing does indeed convey a sense of place. Not necessarily a geographical place, some quaintly-named Nebraska village or shady Niobrara riverbank, but a place nevertheless, with a certain "feel"—a distinctive ethos—about it that assures the reader of the sheer authenticity—the internal, psychological credibility—of what has been written. The literary (and the literary-critical) industry in America has routinely denigrated this sort of writing, condescendingly calling it "regional" writing. As if the supposed alternative—something one supposes they'd call "universal" or even "global" writing—were superior by virtue of its emptiness of real place, of authentic voice, of indwelling spirit. The more one ventures away from place—in writing or in thought— the more one loses direction. It is against this directionless, this slipping from anchor and drifting with the current (of popular "taste" perhaps), that "small" presses like Sandhills pit their energies.

And successfully, the struggles notwithstanding. Sandhills Press has meant much to all of us who have appeared in its pages, not just for another line on the resumé, but for the endorsement of a different brand of individuality that being published there constitutes. A place, in other words, where one can have a place—and be welcomed. And have one's work put before a readership that is not facelessly universal but palpably individual—and individualistic. This is the value of all such presses, not just for the authors whom they find, advocate and serve but also for the readers who can go to their pages for something that they will not find elsewhere. It is in such places—and such presses—that one tastes the literary salt that enhances all the other flavors of the literary world. And, happily, it is also the fresh, pungent pepper.

℘

BIRD POINT

It was there when we felled the old cottonwood,
there, waist-high in a cross section
of the heavy, banded trunk: arrowhead
of black obsidian, buried deep in the heartwood,
embraced by the rings and sheaths
the years had wrapped around it.
Edges fine and flaked with care,
tangs whole and sharp,
it rested as in a lined red palm,
fragile, alien black stone shining its slow passage eastward,
traded from hand to hand, nation to nation,
from Glass Buttes toward the Otoe morning,

until a stray shot left it lodged in a young trunk.

A chance cut disclosed what had been hid:
the tree-man's saw an inch this way or that,
my splitting maul struck to either side,
this pure black point might have lain unseen.
The earth keeps her secrets,
holding near her heart the points and fractures,
stray shots and true, death and silence.
We find what we find, wondering.

The earth reclaims her own, folding
pliant limbs about the fallen fence-rows,
the homesteads left and lifeless that subside
into bindweed and fieldgrass,
wrapping her wounds as the oyster does its hurt
by smoothing the sharp and cutting edges
with round and secret luminescence,
as the frosts and sun consume the boards
that framed a home abandoned,
as the cottonwood took in this small, dark point,
embracing and encircling with soft concentric rings
its sharp obsidian angles.

COYOTE

It's mid-afternoon, and a coyote, tan
as the dust of fallen aspen leaves,
is crossing the west pasture, eyeing me
as he runs, head curled back
over the right shoulder, trusting
the way is clear and straight ahead.

The dry brome strokes his sides,
his underbelly, his upcurved muzzle:
I watch it bend, wave and wake,
as his slender body parts the shafts.

Later this same coyote (we will know him

by his ragged ear) will cross the wrong field,
unwary, strike a fresh diagonal across
a neighbor's backlot filled with wildflowers,
with sage and mullein, spiderwort.
The first shot downs him, tearing
through left flank, soft ivory undercoat,
shatters the pelvis so he cannot stand.
Half-submerged amid the flowers,
he digs front claws into warm clay, draws
his body forward toward the rising moon.

The second shot fills the silence
of late September, expanding in the quiet
like thunder unanticipated; the second shot
shatters his skull, ruins the butter-colored fur,
the deep and glossy pupils behind grey lids
that will not rise again. The second shot
hangs in the air, brooding over the sharp
cry it cannot wholly silence.

SNOW GEESE

The snow geese are moving north,
passing in the dark, their high voices
sifting down like the last heavy snow
that arrives while we sleep.
This is not deep night, though,
but early dark: only nine
and the city still alive but unaware
of what is passing above.
Walking across campus, I hear them,
look up, locate them against the sky,
the stars, the few low broken clouds bearing south
against the motion of these geese.

This is the wild, the elemental,
this chorus of voices self-impelled,
bodies borne easily on wings that work
more rapidly than the great Canada's,

whose fame exceeds these pale, elusive forms.
Through the deep of windy, snowless winter,
the clinging heat of airless prairie summer,
there is no thought of snow geese: it is as though
they were not, neither flying nor calling.

Then, on this sharp March night, this apparition:
this high and fleeting song of night.

Elsewhere, a young family lies dying
in the tangled wreckage of their Plymouth,
crushed at an unmarked crossing;
a junior-high couple makes love
in the bed of his absent parents
who work at night at the Goodyear plant;
a fire creeps undetected through seventy-year-old walls
on Sumner Street, where the brittle wires
have finally bared, touched and ignited;
the Fennertys' seventh son,
who will be Peter, sucks first breath
as he dives headlong from the birth canal;
a poet tricks and prods his words
like white Lippizaners in the ring,
filling pages in careful script.

The snow geese fly on into the night,
above it all, riding a shell of firmament
that surrounds the earth like a case,
revolving suspended,
neither touching nor intersecting
stars or grave, city or sensation.

J.V. Brummels ℰꝺ

J.V. Brummels grew up on farms and ranches in northern Nebraska. He is the descendent of pioneers who first came to the region in the 1870s. Brummels was educated at the University of Nebraska-Lincoln and Syracuse University. He teaches at Wayne State College (from which his grandfather flunked out), where he edited *Nebraska Territory* and directed the Plains Writers Circuit. His poems have appeared in *Chariton Review*, *Quarterly West*, *The Midwest Quarterly*, *Prairie Schooner*, and elsewhere. His books include *614 Pearl* (Abattoir Editions, 1986), *Deus Ex Machina* (Spectra/Bantam, 1989), *Sunday's Child* (Basfal, 1994), *Clay Hills* (Nosila Press, 1996), and *The Cheyenne Line and Other Poems* (Backwaters Press, 2001).

J. V. was co-editor of *On Common Ground* and of the first six volumes of the Plains Poetry Series. "Apple Harvest" and "The One or the Other" appeared in *The PlainSense of Things: Eight Poets from Outstate Nebraska* (1997); "The Damps" in *The Decade Dance* (1991); "What Be and Ain't in Omaha" in *The PlainSense of Things, 3: A Tribute to Larry Holland* (1999); and, "Red Suspenders" in *The Sandhills & Other Geographies: An Anthology of Nebraska Poetry* (1980).

Note from Brummels About Sandhills Press: From the Margins

When I was an undergraduate psychology major at a local university—about two blocks from here—my professors taught me about standard deviations from the mean. I found that term, especially the "deviation" part, intriguing. I still do. What I remember about that education is that behaviors, values, interests—any human activity or belief, really—tend to be grouped along a "normal curve," that about two-thirds of all folks fall within one standard deviation from the average, pretty much agreeing with each other about pretty much everything. Surrounding these folks bunched up like sheep in the middle is the second standard deviation, and that one catches almost all the remainder of us. When we move beyond the second—if we dare—we find about one percent of the human population. It's at these very edges of humanity that we find Hell's Angels, cowboys, crazies, artists and writers. It was about this time in my life that I discovered my passion for poetry.

Poets are marginalized, but it's "not such a bad place to be" (to quote Bill Kloefkorn). The population's a little sparse, but what company there is, is excellent. I met Mark Sanders and Sandhills Press thirty years ago when we were both young poets. Exceedingly young poets. We don't see each other often, but we stay in touch, and there are opportunities like this—a volume celebrating Sandhills Press's 30 years' existence. That's a long time, especially this far from the norm.

Not only has Mark written fine poetry (I particularly recommend his *Here in the Big Empty*), but he's done that thing that most experienced poets draw away from in fear—he's edited and published the work of other poets. I haven't done a scientific study, but I've been around publishers for a long time, and I bet the life expectancy of a small, literary press is somewhere just short of one book. It is a tremendously challenging enterprise, and Mark has been an active and prolific publisher for decades. In 1980, following Edward Field's seminal *A Geography of Poets*, which did much to dissociate "regional" from "provincial" and make "a local habitation and a name" (to quote Ted Kooser who was quoting Shakespeare) a legitimate critical tool, Mark published *The Sandhills & Other Geographies*, one of the earliest anthologies of Nebraska poets. A couple years later, through his Sandhills Press he published *On Common Ground*, an ambitious critical anthology of four of the state's most respected poets—William Kloefkorn, Ted Kooser, Greg Kuzma and Don Welch. (By the way, in the cover photos they appear exceedingly young). I was happy to help him a little when he launched his Plains Poetry Series back in the day when everyone—well, almost everyone—insisted Nebraska was the Midwest. That series of books ran to a half dozen, I believe, and included one by M.K. Stillwell, one of the editors of the more recent anthology *Nebraska Presence* (Backwaters Press).

The list of Sandhills' contributions to literature is too long to detail here, but it has continued to contribute to the collection and appreciation of poetry, both in and around the region for which it's named and to American poetry generally. I can only thank Sandhills and Sanders for the pleasure they've given me through my writing and reading life.

℘

APPLE HARVEST ALONG THE MISSOURI

Someone or something is holding its breath:
A couple travel silently down the road,
the kids finally quiet in the back seat;
the bank of clouds to the northwest
no longer advances on the sun;
the river pauses for an orange barrel
snagged in branches of a fallen cottonwood;
the breeze is taken in by the orchard;
in a sorting shed a man recalls a fragment
of a tune his father used to whistle,
a woman remembers a poem
she was taught in school.

In a moment the wind comes up in the leaves,
the barrel moves out into the sun and current,
a car turns into the lane to buy cider.
In the shed two hands reach for the same small winesap.

THE DAMPS

Not landlords, just old people
with a proprietary interest
in the place they sold us.

We've been here for years already
and they were here a half-century
before. Sure, they remember

the summers of thirty-six, the year
they were married, and thirty-seven
the years they dried out.

I found this picture in a box
in the loft of the east barn,
and sure, and it's his mother

as a young woman. And the windmill,

sure, there's water beneath. But
once he climbed down the pit

to change the leathers and Mike
Jordan was farming across
the road, though road was too

good a word for it, and stopped
his team to come tell him
to watch out for the damps.

Check with a lantern, he said,
for poison air, wave a five-gallon
bucket around to circulate good

with bad. Oh, he'd never heard
of the damps till Mike Jordan,
and I'd never heard till now,

but now when I go down into the pit
I'll know. I got no desire to climb,
I say, into a hole I can't climb out of.

Or a box, he says, thinking,
I suppose, of the picture I found.
Or a box, I say, knowing what he means.

THE ONE OR THE OTHER

1

It's warm enough for rain or cold enough to snow.
It's show up late for work or speed on ice.
It's strap on a belt or keep it coiled.
It's good tracking or a bad spot,
hold her straight on or it's the ass-end coming around,
gaining on you. Through the windshield
the measured pan of your life's country,
the truck you see or you don't see,
the leg-shivering adrenaline of another near-miss
or the audible snap of the bones in your neck.

2

It's the ice and snow that kills you,
but by funeral afternoon it's gallons
of run-off rilling down cemetery hill.
It's life and death in a pulse of weather.
It's live or die and of course it's both.

3

It's go hard on short cold days and sit long
by the stove on these dark-as-night nights.
Or it's just rest in Grandma Ida's rocker
and try to stare the weather down, cloudy or clear.
It's either get up and move around
or get sucked into the fire.

4

Dad's bringing Ruby down to the sale-ring Saturday.
He says, *She ain't good for nothing anymore*
but only for the French to eat. It's keep her
around for nothing or sell her for what
I can get. It's the one or the other. What was
once a pretty roan filly will be hanging,
tendon-hooked meat by the first of the week.

5

Dad's late, or I'm early.
Either way I have time to scout the pens.
Kim's buying tack before running up
to the gun show to find a holster.
It was his old bird guns or a three-fifty-seven,
and along his share of the river
they've had some shooting scrapes.
It's scattershot or revolvers,
guns or knives, stones or clubs.
The ridges of my country's repopulated,
cracker meatpackers come north to work
the new plants. I know it's follow the work
or go hungry. Still, a few months
of finding strangers where friends used to live,
of cut linefences, of road signs tattooed

with an assault rifle's forty-round clip,
a time or two of coming out of bed all of a once
with late-night headlights raking the house,
has got me thinking it's the one fear or the other.

6
My wife's uncle Burdette's in ill-health,
bones too brittle to fall down on,
his voice too feeble to carry two feet,
so Aunt Viola belled him for emergencies
with a whistle. He blows it now
at family get-togethers just to get her goat.
It's either that or sit on his hands.

7
This is the place to buy or sell
and I've bought nothing to rid myself of.
I sit on my hands awhile. At the chutes,
Dad's unloading Ruby, late because
in the thirteen years they've run that horse
no one's thought to trailer-break her.
She had to be roped in against her will.
Either that or let her run the river
till natural causes took her, the whore.
Oh, she's a whore of the Elkhorn Valley, alright,
a hell-bitch who broke my brother's arm
and nose, who piled me in the river.

8
I've neighbored a few whores,
sat a horse on my own range
and watched the johns arrive
in cars stripped of plates.
The kids, only a little younger,
hunker in the side
yard around trash fires
while their mothers play for pay.

9
Everything has its price,

they say. Maybe
this is my native tongue,
the amplified litany of haggle,
my priest the auctioneer.

10
Or:
Before matter breathed
only energy awaiting a name
roamed the void,
and all enhancement
trailing it down through time
is only riffs
on that profound groan.

11
Or:
The way it was to start,
the prophet says,
it's going to be again.
Here, then, is prophecy for us all.
The swinging dick of rhythm
makes its natural way back down
to the single, attenuated syllable,
the *hy-up!* of bidders doing business.
Even a great poem's blue-sky-arching
shout falls to the rocks. Past
the high-tide of human speech,
a mute community waits.

12
Only principle devolves to choice.
It's the one or the other,
to live or to die,
to whore or to love,
my dad's limp towards me or my son's quick run away,
to be struck dumb or blow a whistle,
my folks' tongue or the speech of strangers,
to sit on my hands or grunt a nonsense bid.

13
What the hell. I choose
the last of a string of tall colts,
a gray. I give the man
my number and my money.
I take my chances
on a horse I name Red Jack.

RED SUSPENDERS

Red, all right—what I'd expect from a scarlet
tanager's wings in mating time.
Perhaps someday in some season
I'll see one. Today I looked
as much as I ever do, driving
up highway fifteen
to the junction with twenty, taking gravel roads
after that, just as colorless
in the sun as the concrete, with dark arcs
here and there from irrigation that's
overshot its field. The brome in the ditches melts
into the deeper green of row after row
of com and beans. Even in the pastures

the cows graze in rows, heading, as always,
in one direction (today it's southeast).
In one place they are faced, from across
a fence, by hay bales going northwest in a field that seems too closely
cropped to recover. There are lines
less straight—the green willows that follow
the irregular coursings of some small
water we call a creek but in less
arid country would carry no name.
Here the Department of Roads announces them:
Bogus and Logan, Dry Gulch and Papillion.
Who knows what Frenchman happened a century
and a half
ago to die or piss on this spot?

Where I imagine him standing
there's a white cat in tall grass that
erases his eyes with common color. His pause
tells me though he's watching something.
I snap my brand-new suspenders,
red as blood, wide as July,
just received from a mail order house
in Maine, and laugh hard from deep in myself.
The cat loses his color and disappears.

WHAT BE AND AIN'T IN OMAHA

Old Greener Ford truck be riding high wide and handsome
down Dodge above Beemers and Volvers
carrying certifiable republican accountants
and constipated shoelick-clerks
and wives turned out too nice for the dentist
sinning maybe their Friday afternoon away.

When northern boys come to town ain't for fast food
nor the Westroads nor the Crossroads nor the Regency Court
cause K-Mart by any name be just a store
and northern boys ain't buying.

What ain't no longer be the Stockyards cause
some pandering Chamber of Commerce son of a bitch
cemented over where the sweat
of Swedes and Germans and Blacks and Irish and Poles
stewed in the blood of Sandhills beeves
and Wobblies got a foothold
and a Union man'd blackjack a scab sooner'd spit.

What be be a parking lot but what ain't
be a space for Greener Ford
but northern boys be moving a sign to make one
and what be be nobody the wiser nor the poorer for it.
Ain't no perfect cup of coffee inside neither
and neither can northern boys find no gambling
and chicken ranches all be rumor in the smog.

Northern boys be in a fever for George Dickel and dish water
feeding straight through the hotel faucet pipes
right out of the Big River which ain't a branch of nothing
cause the Mississippi only be an upstream fork
and only the maps ain't be yet corrected.

Northern boys be
trimming American language
till only form of be
be be
and pretty soon
pretty women be
making a loop
to see northern boys be
making loose
change disappear
inside a Balleyhat

and if someone
be needing a hanging
a rope be handy
but mostly the peoples
let northern boys be
cause they be knowing
Mister Smith and Mister Wesson
personal. And when northern boys
spit or piss
the Big River
be swelling out
of its downstream banks.

*

When northern boys be waking up
in hotel room it be cans and bottles
be rolling off their blankets
to the floorrug. And northern boys ain't
be so cocky now. Old Greener Ford be
hitting every pothole on Dodge but
pretty soon Old Greener's tail be wagging

to the city be reminding northern boys
fresh spirits be handy in the glovebox.
Northern boys be leaving lighthearted

because northern boys be
and all that be
be northern boys
and what ain't
be of no consequence.

(for Larry Holland and Paul "Red" Shuttleworth)

KELLY CHERRY ❧

Kelly Cherry was born in Baton Rouge, Louisiana. She received a B.A. from Mary Washington College and an M.F.A. from the University of North Carolina at Greensboro. She published her first work of fiction, *Sick and Full of Burning*, in 1974, closely followed by her first collection of poetry, *Love and Agnostics*, in 1975. Her most recent books are *Girl in a Library: On Women Writers & the Writing Life* (BkMk, 2009), and *Retreats of Thoughts: Poems* (LSU, 2009). Kelly Cherry lives in Virginia.

"The Poem" was published in the Main-Traveled Roads Chapbook series in 1999.

NOTE FROM CHERRY ABOUT SANDHILLS PRESS

After I wrote "The Poem: An Essay," I wasn't sure what to do with it. I might have submitted it to a journal as a piece of prose—which is what it is—but its use of repetition and rhythm and its dismissal of ordinary transitions would, I thought, drive an editor of prose bonkers. Its length, I thought, would make it ineligible for most poetry publications, and besides, it wasn't a poem. It just sometimes resembled a poem, just as it sometimes resembled a story or autobiography without being either. Then I thought of Mark Sanders.

Mark had previously published a couple of my poems in his excellent literary journal *Hurakan*. Something of mine had also appeared in an anthology he produced called *The Decade Dance: A Celebration of Poems*. Indeed, as editor of Sandhills Press he has edited and produced several invaluable anthologies that collect Midwestern writing. He also published chapbooks. I sent my essay to him and was thrilled when he offered to bring it out as a chapbook. Prose chapbooks are not as widely current today as are poetry chapbooks, and I knew I was lucky to have found him.

I admire Mark's own fiction and poetry (read *Here in the Big Empty!*) and am deeply grateful for his support of my work. He and his wife, Kimberly Verhines, have pursued their own writing while initiating and managing the journal and Sandhills Press with its two imprints, Main-Traveled Roads Press and Lewis-Clark Press. (And teaching!) To think that this anthology marks the thirtieth anniversary of Sandhills is breathtaking. It is a tribute to the Press and especially to Mark's determination and his devotion to the idea of independent publishing.

I should add that "his" writers compose a varied group to which I am honored to belong. It includes such esteemed poets as Don Welch and William Kloefkorn. Many of these writers are voices of the Plains and the Midwest, voices that need to be more often heard in the United States—and are heard, thanks to a Press that takes care to curate and present them. Mark has a large vision for literature and publishing that includes us all (and places Midwestern writers where they belong—at the center).

ॐ

THE POEM

Perhaps the poem can be anything, but it must be something. It requires a shape.

The poem is a shape describing itself in time.

Like music, the poem is a passage. The reader enters and exits.

Necessarily, therefore, the poem is not without beginning and end.

The lyric, which attempts to arrest a single moment, contradicts itself, wherein lies its poignancy.

Thus the poem is a representation of time sculpted in eternity. The poet carves a shape in eternity, and the shape is time.

The poem is an object, an *objet d'art*. It takes many forms.

The poet makes an object that will speak to a reader.

The reader's communion is with the poem, not the poet.

Or—there is more than one way to do (not just say) the above—the poet builds the poem.

The better poet breathes the poem. The poem must be able, finally, to breathe on its own.

The poem wants to appear on the page and is only waiting to see if you, too, wish it to appear on the page.

I stayed up nights, writing. I was in love with the poem, it was the only company I needed.

I heard the poem as a kind of music, but it was more than shaped sound (as is music, of course). Beyond the music of the words lay the music of meaning, the sweetest music I ever heard.

Other nights, I walked through the city, Knoxville or New York or Moscow. The streets were still black-damp from rain, and traffic lights glistened. I had a cream-colored leather coat with a belt that tied, and I cinched the belt tighter.

In Knoxville, in the diner, the juke box played rock-and-roll or country-western songs.

I was alone in the booth in the diner.

The poem longs to be written. It does not care whether it is read. It is by being written that the poem knows it is loved.

Everything that lives longs to be loved, the girl in the diner, the girl at her desk, the poem.

The poem loves you. It is like God in this, loving you simply because you are yourself and thought of it. You must treat it with respect and tenderness.

Poetry requires a quietening of the heart. There must be a surrounding space of time, clear of anxiety and anger, a margin of pure space around the self's sheet of paper. This is why more time is needed to write poetry than fiction.

Life will not enter the poem until self-regard has left it.

The poem comes fully into being as the poet surrenders her own sense of being. Room must be cleared for the poem.

Often enough, I wrote happy poems when I was sad, and sad poems when I was happy.

Meanwhile, the city was glowing with liquid fire, the way the lights from the cars, traffic lights, street lamps, marquees, the lights of restaurants and bars wavered on wet window panes, dark puddles, the sides of passing buses.

Everyone was pushing against everyone. Because they wanted to get there first, or they wanted to be noticed, or both.

She–that one there, then–turned the corner, scaled a flight of stairs.

She stood naked, at his request, under the bare light bulb. He had said he thought he might paint her portrait. She wanted him to love her, but she had no idea what love is.

His rented room was above a Chinese restaurant. Although the room was quiet, it was full of loud smells–dough, ginger, green tea.

He turned her this way and that, examining her beneath the light. Her heart beat against her chest, begging to be let out, so shy it wanted to run away.

He decided against painting her portrait. Her leather coat was still lying on top of the fold-out cot.

Before she left, when he wasn't looking, she reached inside her chest, brought out her heart, and set it on the piano.

The heart of the poem is a rose in a vase on a piano.
Poem is a rose is a poem.

On the street again, she again wrapped her belt around her tightly. The wind had picked up its pace, the night was colder.

Why I stayed up through the night: Writing poetry is a way of thinking. If it were not, it would be miniature golf, Tic-Tac-Toe, a game of Go Fish. Poems would be dolls, Barbie dolls, baby dolls, Raggedy Ann dolls. The poet would dress the doll in different outfits: Barbie waiting for the Westron winde to blow, the smalle raine to raine downe, Barbie on moon-blanch'd Dover Beach; Barbie attired for woodlands where cherry trees are hung with snow. When the poem is alive, it dresses itself. It becomes itself. (It has style.)

Thinking keeps a person awake.

When I looked up from my worktable, it was 4 A.M., and the classical station was playing Hindemith. The sky had begun to lighten. Most of the stars had disappeared.

What I tried to do, what seemed to me important to do, was to think a thing through.

How does the writer of a poem think? She follows the strongest and deepest connections among words. The connections may be formal or semantic. One metaphor associates itself with another through imagery. Memory and imagination offer suggestions. Haven't you ever written a poem about which you said, afterward, Wait a minute, this is not what I felt! This is not what I believed! But it is, it is, or, more intriguingly, at least it could be. You are surprised—now you know something you did not know before. You know what you are capable of feeling, what you are capable of thinking.

If you are not persuaded of this, the poem fails. Throw it away. Come back to it later.

Writing the poem is like listening to echoes, half echoes.

The painter she went to see in his rented room—I used to remember what he looked like but now I've forgotten.

It was four in the morning. There was a light blue sky lifting toward pink. The world was blushing. She let herself into the house, walked to her own rented room at the back. Beneath sweaters in a drawer was a pint of bootlegged whiskey. Possessing it made her feel a little like an outlaw, which was how she felt anyway, without the whiskey, which she never drank because she hated the taste of it.

She thinks of her heart, how its petals must still be falling like drops of blood onto the polished piano.

Rose is a rose is a poem.

The poem wants to open its heart–to you, to whoever will love it.

A young girl at her desk will entertain herself in any number of ways: writing a poem, drawing a geological time-line, construing Cicero, sorting types of thought under two large headings, LOGIC and ANA-LOGIC. If she can grab a couple of hours' sleep before it's time to leave for school, she is fine. She fixes her own lunch in a brown paper bag, carries it on top of her books and them on top of the three-ring binder.

I remember that that girl, the one in that coat, in that city, had no money for a bus or a cab and walked home from the painter's room. I remember that one of the streets she walked down had streetlights that were like herons standing on one leg, shining heads jutting forward out over the street.

The poem is a rose with thorns.

But you knew that.

It is not unusual for a poem to take twenty or thirty years to complete itself. Patience is key. Even more important is tenacity. You must wait. You must not give up. You must return to the poem again and again.

What the poem loves most about you is your willingness to keep trying.

And the poem is waiting for you to find it. Imagine a poem as simple as a rose-blossom, stem, leaf. Imagine a poem as layered and overlapping as a rose, petals interleaved, leaves like maps (because of their purposeful veining). Follow the poem's own, so green map.

As for the girl in that city– As for her–

As the sun rose higher in the sky, she slipped into bed. She thought she would read. (She was reading *Don Quixote*, one of her father's two favorite books.)

But she thought her father had lost faith in her.

The poem wants to love you. Though it is shy, it is not as shy as you might think.

Poem is a poem is a rose, a heart.

You can spend a lifetime with it. On it.

The poem is waiting for you--in any city or country, anywhere.

I definitely remember that. That she thought her father had lost faith in her.

I came home on the school bus. The girls' field-hockey team, in blue one-piece gym suits with Y-necks and short sleeves and short skirts and under the skirts, sewn-on bloomers, was taking turns hitting practice balls to the goalie, whose brown hair had escaped from the safety mask's backstrap. The wood sticks clicked against the leathern balls. There was a breeze, a bright breeze bearing the glittering gold heat of summer into September's shortening days, and it blew in through the bus's open windows and riffled the pages of the book I was reading.

The poem is always waiting. Even then, it was waiting.

And even then, the days and nights were turning over, tracking each other through the years.

Because I knew this, I was in my room, late at night, working.

Stephen Corey &

Stephen Corey has published nine collections of poems, among them: *There Is No Finished World* (White Pine Press, 2003); *Mortal Fathers and Daughters* (Palanquin Press, 1999); *All These Lands You Call One Country* (University of Missouri Press, 1992); and *Synchronized Swimming* (Swallow's Tale Press, 1985, reissued by Livingston Press, 1993). Corey's poems, essays, and reviews have appeared in many periodicals, among them *Shenandoah, The American Poetry Review, Poetry, The Kenyon Review, The New Republic, Ploughshares, The North American Review, Yankee, Yellow Silk, Poets & Writers, The Laurel Review,* and *The Southern Review.* Since 1983, he has been with *The Georgia Review,* serving variously as assistant editor, associate editor, acting editor, and as of January 1, 2008, editor.

Both of these poems were included in *The Decade Dance* (1991).

&

Complicated Shadows

To hawks we're a woodland insect,
four legs above and four below, twitching
on the ground as if a flash-tongued sun
sought to flicker through us to the spot we've claimed.

Each small move we make is shading for one,
quick burning for the other—our bodies
become one another's clothing tugged off,
wrapped on, stripped away again in glowing haste.

The question of shadows gains depth
when our stomachs press close
to leave no space from skin to skin,
sealing a damp plane between us,
a pressure of pure darkness

we feel but cannot see:
light needs at least a chance to be absent—
no shadows in locked closets,
behind closed lids, within the heart's chambers.

We are weaving and folding, we
know this soil is a great compost heap,
we are making and unmaking
light--forcing the aging hot sun to run.

Taking the Light Whitely

Certain habits can seem miraculous
in the thoughts of the dispossessed:
to have chosen your own clothing
from stores and then your closet,
to have shaven yet again in the mist
dulling your bathroom mirror—
such are the dreams of the homeless...

I rarely consider my fingers or tongue
until slicing or slamming or burning.
Now, I see how the air outlines the air
in every space where you're not.
I see how we let the ways we caressed
mound like seeds in a bushel basket,
uniform, topping off higher and higher
for as long as we could pour.
I see all those mornings by windows,
on beds nearly overflowing
with movements we made and made, and felt
we watched more closely than we did.
Now, we are a history I work to imagine
into every place we were, a chronicle
no others could even think to restore.
And we are a future, scattered across the country
in the separate strings of houses
we will come to occupy with others—
some for many years.

We do not know them yet, there is nothing
familiar in their rooms or air.

And still, each holds today
what will hold when we've come and gone:
shafts of sun on a thin sill, a pine floor,
a stark wall of whatever color--
one space after another
taking the light whitely,
spot after spot illumined
by that which must touch without touching.

FAILURE TO BE PRIESTS: A MODERN HARVEST

> as a stallion stalwart, very-violet-sweet...
> –Gerard Manley Hopkins

If we do not see the horses fraught with flowers,
the musical fire of invisible hummingbirds,
the graceful, loping gait of tombstones crossing fields,
it is from our stagnant fear of mockery--
our worry to be right, and righteous, and exact--
our failure once again, on waking, to be priests.

We know this globe that could be a mushroom
might not be at all--sprouting fast but scarcely quick
into the far blue air we have named God's face--
so now we find that all we can believe
is so much less than all, is shadowed and shackled
by dark and thinning thought, by chains of flimsy logic
closing off the organ's pipes to still
our outrageous music, our glorious tin-turned-to-golden singing.

DAVID DWYER ℰℭ

David Dwyer died of lung cancer in 2003; his first book of poems was *Ariana Olisvos: Her Last Works and Days*, the winner of the 1976 Juniper Prize (published by the University of Massachusetts Press). His second collection, *Other Men and Other Women*, was published by Sandhills Press in 1985. Formerly from New York, he lived the last years of his life between South Dakota and Hawaii. He was married to writer Kathleen Norris.

The poems included here come from *Other Men and Other Women*.

ℰℭ

METAPHYSICS

Once, in a seedy Mafia bar, near where my father
used to live, I saw a woman walk,
in silver shoes and a black G-string, among
empty tables to a silent jukebox. She popped
a quarter in. I turned away, still cold
from the world, where it was snowing. My father was away.
I'd come up from the city to see him. I was 25.
All my childhood, I always knew where both
my parents were, and now I did not. "That
is the difference," I said to myself. And, "Gin," I said
to the bartender, "splash o' tonic."
                                        Rock 'n' roll.
She had begun to dance in the rosy light
across the dark room. Four or five
other men hunched on their stools by the door
and did not look at her or at each other.
I hunched among them, staring in my glass.

I want to say we were ashamed, that for shame
at our silly sex we could not look at her.

But really, I was afraid.
                                    I have made her in memory
a terrifying beauty, golden-skinned,
Diana among low, moonstruck dogs.
But really, I do not know.   I was afraid
to look at her.
                        Three songs and silence
again.   She walked to the far end of the bar
and slipped a dark cloak on, a monk's
robe almost.   In memory I have made it
the color of dried blood, but really I do not
know.   I was afraid to look.
                                    Outside,
it snowed on my childhood, of course, and on the gutted
warehouse across the street.   (Fifteen years
before, I saw it burn, on a snowy night.)

Another quick gin, and I went to take a leak.
I had to walk by her.   She hunched on her stool, her naked
hand propping a book up on the bar.
Also Sprach Zarathustra, I read and turned
away.
            This doesn't sound true, even to me.
Nonetheless, it is the case.   The world
is everything that is the case:
                                    the snow
on my father's empty house, the old geography
I knew by heart, the invisible woman,
rosy light and darkness, German meta-
physics…

            So.   That bar's been gone for years,
and the rundown block of flats behind it I've just
remembered.   "Mark Twain Apartments," it said
above the crooked door that opened on
a dirty hall of which I was afraid.
I don't know where my father is.   I am afraid
of different things these days.   I hope she is happy.
I hope she is however beautiful she cares
to be, however wise, a philosopher,
a woman of the world.

"*Inyàñ wakàñ*,"
an old Lakota woman told me once
in another sleazy bar, in Chamberlain, South
Dakota. "*Oyàte hé wakàñ*." The rocks
are holy. Even this world is holy.

THE RAILROAD STATION AT SABATTIS, NY; 21 JUNE 86

Just about now, just before dawn,
I got off the train here alone,
as deep in the forest as any road runs.
Both of my parents
hung in the mist, awaiting me.
It was nineteen-sixty-one. No one
had ever died, and the sun was rising.

The rails run blood-brown now; they will never again
bring anyone home. People were paid,
back in the sixties, to strip
the station, break
the windows out, and sweep up after.
They did it as men do such things,
so the wreck looks deliberate,
but not quite finished.

                         Inside, ribbed hardwood
glows on the waiting-room walls. It is
not even dusty. The last deliberate
hand to touch it was trying to be kind,
saying goodbye with wax and lemon oil.

And the mist is the same. The clatter
of birds and bullfrogs from the swamp
across the track is just the same—

People can sometimes guess
where they have to go. I will never again
have to come here.

I start the car
and crank the tape-deck up:
Dear Janis Joplin,
who died in the dark of heroin
a thousand years ago—
                    Here, it is the first dawn
after the solstice. The sun
is rising in the mist. Everyone
dies. Deep in the enchanted forest,
she is singing "Summertime."

To Kathleen, with a Rabbit

 Yes, I have noticed the ghost in the kitchen. I knew
she would be there. And something rustles through
the long, lavendered closet between their bedrooms
when I kick off the engineer boots I bought
on 14th Street, in another life.
                                   Her machine
gagged on sixty seasons' fur and feathers
when I washed that old canvas hunting jacket,
washed your grandfather's bloody fingerprints
away, in the house he built in nineteen-ten.

It fits me, very nearly. The man who farms
the land he thought was his forever knew it.
"I'd 'a' knowed that coat 'n' a bear 'as wearin' it,
leave alone you," he said. He seemed to think
that washing it was, all things told, all right.
Odd, perhaps, but no offense. Wearing it,
likewise. A ghost in the cottonwood grove by the shrinking
pond seemed to nod.

                    (Another man has told me
that once, in a cooler Fall, when he was young
and the pond full, he spoke with an old Lakota
soldier in that stand of trees one sunset.
"Can't rightly promise 'f he 'as alive…had on
a Ghost Dance shirt, color o'sky 'n' water,

should'a' been in the Cody *museum*. But, LORD, he could talk.
Talk the ears offn a deef man 'n' ramble
right along—*he* di'n' care...")

        In the breaks
to the south, this afternoon, by your grandfather's
pasture, his old friend just missed a hard, running
shot at a fox -- a dribble of rust across
the draw wiped suddenly away. "There's thirty,
maybe forty bucks there, gone t'ground.
Ah, come first snow 'n' he's fat 'n' furry, maybe
fifty—he'll be mine."
    His rifle's high
snap and its echo, anyway, spooked this fat
cottontail. My right hand drew my heavy
single-action Ruger out; my left
closed 'round and cocked the pistol.
       (I was thinking
of something else entirely.)
       I cocked my head;
his fields, the rabbit, the whole universe moved,
while I stared down the fixed sights, took
a deep breath in; we froze, relaxed; I squeezed
the trigger.
     (I had been thinking how odd it is
that nearly all the quite sufficient store
of things I own, a few guns left aside,
is made of paper.)
      I killed this rabbit, then,
though I cannot say I know who owns it. Soon --
since it must be wrong to kill even a rabbit
you mean to eat with less than your whole heart
and mind engaged—soon I shall have to give up
either blood-sport or daydreams...
       For this rabbit, however,
the matter's academic. Tonight, in your grandmother's
thoughtful kitchen, I'll make it ours with her well-
used tools and a foreign recipe I noted down,
in another life.
     I cannot say that I know

all their land is talking about, less
still what their talky old house has in mind. I'd just
as soon live with those voices, though, till
I can hear them.
                              Today, while he thought the cottontail
had me absorbed, I caught in the corner of my eye
a harmless blacksnake, the color of printer's ink,
scribbling another man's name in the papery grass.
I know what he means. Odd, perhaps, but no
offense. No offense meant. None taken.

Baling Wheatstraw on My 33rd Birthday

Between fallow and fallow, the mile-long strips
of stubble ten-rods-wide surrender

each from two hundred and fifty to four hundred
bales to the spring-steel fingers and close-
mouthed jaws of the loud, fast-talking machine.

Stubble-by-, stubble-by-, stubble-by-fallow, it says
in the light straw on the hilltops and *She wouldn't, she wouldn't.*
she won't, going down the draws. My old Eight-Forty
John Deere tractor asks me, *But wh'd'y'*
know? But wh'd'y'know? She might…

                              Riding
the clutch in the thick bottom-land, I lose
all track of their talk, tractor and baler both chattering,
both snarling nonsense.
                              (A golden eagle helped me
seed this field last spring and ate three mice
and gophers I unconvered; now a misquided
sea-gull follows me, an easy symbol
of exile and high hopes.)
                              Hopes, the tractor
mutters, beginning to climb the draw. *Hopes,*
slopes, ropes, learn the ropes. The baler
answers: *Even…even the, even the, even the birds*

can fly.

      The dead, the tractor snapes, *the dead, even the*
dead…Even the birds…(They have begun
to argue, it is so steep.) *Even the dead…*
Now, doesn't it? Even the…Doesn't it? Even the birds
can fly. Even the dead . . . But, doesn't it? doesn't it?
Even the dead can lie down. But, doesn't it? doesn't it
make you feel old? Well, you are. You are.

After the War: a vision for Kathleen

The sickness will come to all of us, out of the air:
we will have poisoned what we live in -- a thing
no rat would ever do. That nasty book
of Nevil Shute's will turn out true, and even
the worst imaginings of Orwell and of Aldous Huxley
will seem utopian ...
      Despairingly, we'll sort through the proverbs:
a cat will still be able to look at a king,
but no one will know the way to the dairy, no one
will tell the emperor the truth, or hear the truth
if it is spoken.
      It will not be spoken. Privately,
each of us will absorb what she must. The pot
of gold at rainbow's end will be radioactive
and death to touch; the miraculous child will not
be born; disappointment will spread, will become the natural
state of things. Expecting a message, a few of us
will look to the violent sky; believing in reason,
a few will write strictly accurate accounts of the sickness.
Still, the sickness will come to us all: to the young,
the beautiful, the cheerleaders and the quarterbacks, the ill-
at-ease, the all-too-confident…
      At the very end,
simple kindness may still count for something; unable
to help each other ("Could we ever?"), we'll share
morphine and alcohol and silly jokes.
I hope I will have the strength to wipe the blood
and sweat and so on from your face and lie to you.

I hope you may do the same for me. The others
will ask each other: "Did we win? Did we win?" I hope
that you and I will know.

MORAL PHILOSOPHY IN AUGUST

A woman set her cool, brown back
against the fingertips of my right hand.
We were dancing.
                    Dear flesh I guess I'll never
know as well as I might like to, dear,
I hope you are happy in the children, half our age,
I cannot imagine having come from between
those young legs, and in the husband
I find it almost as hard to imagine as my
imaginary wife.
                    Now we have changed the summer
place we met in, only by leaving it, into
a place where no one lives, I hope you will be
happy all summers (weak as these words are)
and your flesh more at ease than my fingers were.

B. H. FAIRCHILD ℰ

B. H. Fairchild grew up in small towns in Texas, Oklahoma, and southwest Kansas. He is the author of *The Arrival of the Future*, *Local Knowledge*, and *The Art of the Lathe*, a finalist for the National Book Award and winner of the Kingsley Tufts Award, the William Carlos Williams Award, the California Book Award, the PEN Center West Poetry Award, and an award from the Texas Institute of Letters. He is the recipient of Guggenheim, Rockefeller/Bellagio, and NEA Fellowships, and received the Arthur Rense Poetry Award from the American Academy of Arts and Letters.

The two poems included here were published in *The Decade Dance* (1991).

ℰ

THE STRUCTURES OF EVERYDAY LIFE

In the shop's nave, where the wind bangs sheets
of tin against iron beams, barn sparrows
quarrel like old lovers. At five o'clock
the lathes wind down from their long flight.
Burnt coils of steel loom from collecting bins.

In the wash room photographs of wives and lovers
look down on the backs of men pale as shells.
Brown wrists and black hands lather and shine
in the light of one dim lamp, and blue shirts
hang like the stilled hands of a deaf-mute.

When the foreman sees his raw face in the mirror,
he turns away, shy as a young girl, sick of iron
and rust, the dead sun of the day's end. After
washing, his wet hair gleams in the open door
and he begins his dream of women in cool rooms.

Gusts seep through tin, making the thin music
the men live by. Drill pipe they scar knuckles on
clangs restless as planets on the rack outside.
The ten-ton hoist drags its death chain. The sky
is a gray drum, a dull hunger only the plains know.

Like children at prayer, the men kneel to lace
their shoes, touching the worn heels of a life.
When they leave, the faces on their locker doors
turn back to darkness. Each man shoulders the sun,
carries it through the fields, the lighted streets

THERE IS A CONSTANT MOVEMENT IN MY HEAD

*The choreographer from Nebraska
is listening to her mother's cane
hammering the dance floor, down, down,
like some gaunt, rapacious bird
digging at a rotted limb. The mother
still beats time in her daughter's head.*

There is constant movement in my head,
the choreographer begins. In Nebraska
I learned to dance and guilt from my mother,
held my hands out straight until the cane
beat my palms blue. I was a wild bird
crashing into walls, calming down

only to dance. When Tallchief came down
from New York, a dream flew into my head:
to be six feet tall, to dance the *Firebird*
all in black and red, to shock Nebraska
with my naked, crazy leaps until the cane
shook in the furious hand of my mother.

Well, that day never came. My mother
thought I could be whittled down,
an oak stump to carve into some cane

she could lean on. But in my head
were the sandhill cranes that crossed Nebraska
each fall: sluggish, great-winged birds

lumbering from our pond, the air bird-
heavy with cries and thrumming. My mother
knew. She said I would leave Nebraska,
that small-town life could only pull me down.
Then her hands flew up around her head
and she hacked at the air with her cane.

There are movements I can't forget: the cane
banging the floor, dancers like huge birds
struggling into flight, and overhead,
the choreography of silver cranes my mother
always watched when the wind blew down
from the sandhills and leaves fell on Nebraska.

This dance is the cane of my mother.
The dancers are birds that will never come down.
They were all in my head when I left Nebraska.

DANA GIOIA ℰℴ

Former Chairman of the National Endowment for the Arts, Dana Gioia is an internationally acclaimed and award-winning poet. A native Californian of Italian and Mexican descent, Gioia received a B.A. and a M.B.A. from Stanford University and an M.A. in Comparative Literature from Harvard University. His poetry collection, *Interrogations at Noon*, won the 2002 American Book Award. An influential critic as well, Gioia's 1991 *Can Poetry Matter?*, a finalist for the National Book Critics Circle award, is credited with helping to revive the role of poetry in American public culture. His poems, translations, essays, and reviews have appeared in many magazines including *The New Yorker, The Atlantic, The Washington Post Book World, The New York Times Book Review, Slate*, and *The Hudson Review*.

"The Anonymity of the Regional Poet," the essay which follows this note, first appeared in *On Common Ground: The Poetry of William Kloefkorn, Ted Kooser, Greg Kuzma, and Don Welch*, which Sandhills published in 1983. Gioia's essay astutely prophesizes Ted Kooser's forthcoming success.

ℰℴ

THE ANONYMITY OF THE REGIONAL POET

1. The Predicament Of Popular Poetry

> Ordinary thoughts and feelings are not necessarily
> shallow, any more than subtle or unusual ones are
> necessarily profound.
>
> — Edwin Muir

Ted Kooser is a popular poet. This is not to say that he commands a mass public. No contemporary poet does – at least in America. Kooser is popular in that unlike most of his peers he writes naturally for a nonliterary public. His style is accomplished but extremely simple – his diction drawn from common speech, his syntax conversational. His subjects are chosen from the everyday world of the Great Plains, and his sensibility, though more subtle and articulate, is that of the average Midwesterner. Kooser never makes an allusion that an intelligent but unbookish reader will not immediately grasp. There is to my knowledge no poet of equal stature who writes so convincingly in a manner the average American can understand and appreciate.

But to describe Kooser merely as a poet who writes plainly about the ordinary world is misleading insofar as it makes his work sound dull. For here, too, the comparison with popular art holds true. Kooser is uncommonly entertaining. His poems are usually short and perfectly paced, his subjects relevant and engaging. Finishing one poem, the reader instinctively wants to proceed to another. It has been Kooser's particular genius to develop a genuine poetic style that accommodates the average reader and portrays a vision that provides unexpected moments of illumination from the seemingly threadbare details of everyday life.

If Kooser's work is visionary, however, it is on a decidedly human scale. He offers no blinding flashes of inspiration, no mystic moments of transcendence. He creates no private mythologies or fantasy worlds. Instead he provides small but genuine insights into the world of everyday experience. His work strikes the difficult balance between profundity and accessibility, just as his style manages to be personal without being idiosyncratic. It is simple without becoming shallow, striking without going to extremes. He has achieved the most difficult kind of originality. He has transformed the common idiom and experience into fresh and distinctive poetry.

But what does an instinctively popular poet do in contemporary America, where serious poetry is no longer a popular art? The public whose values and sensibility he celebrates is unaware of his existence. Indeed, even if they were aware of his poetry, they would feel no need to approach it. Cut off from his proper audience, this poet feels little sympathy with the specialized minority readership that now sustains poetry either as a highly sophisticated verbal game or secular religion. His sensibility shows little similarity to theirs except for the common interest in poetry. And so the popular poet usually leads a marginal existence in literary life. His fellow poets look on him as an anomaly or anachronism. Reviewers find him eminently unnewsworthy. Publishers see little prestige attached to printing his work. Critics, who have been trained to celebrate complexity, consider him an amiable simpleton.

It is not surprising then that Kooser's work has not received sustained attention from academic critics. In an age when serious critics have begun to look on themselves either as creative personalities hardly less important than the authors they discuss or at the very least as great interpretive artists – the Van Cliburns of poetry – without whose skilled touch literature would remain as mute as an unopened score, there is little in Kooser's work that would summon forth a great performance. There are no problems to solve, no ambiguities to unravel, no dizzying bravado passages to master for the dexterous critic eager to earn an extra curtain call. What can a critic meaningfully add to the attentive reader's appreciation of this poem, for instance, which is one of Kooser's more-complex pieces:

The Blind Always Come As Such A Surprise

The blind always come as such a surprise,
suddenly filling an elevator
with a great white porcupine of canes,
or coming down upon us in a noisy crowd
like the eye of a hurricane.
The dashboards of cars stopped at crosswalks
and the shoes of commuters on trains
are covered with sentences
struck down in mid-flight by the canes of the blind.
Each of them changes our lives,
tapping across the bright circles of our ambitions
like cracks traversing the favorite china.

One can enumerate its small beauties – the opening image of a blind person (or persons) entering an elevator to the slight alarm of other passengers, the unexpectedly surreal equation of a porcupine's quills and the white tipped canes, the sharp observations of how normal people pause uncomfortably when they notice the blind or disabled, the rhetorical trick of referring to the blind collectively, which gives them a mysterious, sexless, ageless composite identity, or the haunting final simile. But aside from cataloguing these moments, there is little a critic can provide that the average reader cannot, because the difficulties this poem provokes are experiential rather than textual. It poses none of the verbal problems critical methodologies have been so skillfully designed to unravel. Rather it quietly raises certain moral and psychological issues that the professional critic by training is not prepared to engage or resolve.

Paradoxically, the simpler poetry is, the more difficult it becomes for a critic to discuss intelligently. Trained to explicate, the critic often loses the ability to evaluate literature outside the critical act. A work is good only in proportion to the richness and complexity of interpretations it provokes. Finding little challenge in Kooser's poetry, the enterprising critic is tempted to dismiss it. Surely poetry so simple must lack depth. While admitting to a certain superficial fascination, the critic qualifies his admiration by exploring the author's limitations, which in itself becomes a compelling critical activity. While defining a poet's limitations is a legitimate critical pursuit, limitations in themselves are not necessarily short-comings. Even the greatest authors have blind spots: Milton had little gift for comedy; Wordsworth a relatively narrow technical range. To find a limitation does not necessarily invalidate an author's achievement. Criticism should make meaningful distinctions, not apply irrelevant standards.

Kooser does have significant limitations as a poet. Looking across all his mature work, one sees a narrow range of technical means, an avoidance of stylistic or thematic complexity, little interest in ideas, and an unwillingness to work in longer forms. In his weaker poems one also notices a tendency to sentimentalize his subjects and too strong a need to be liked by his readers, which expresses itself in a self-deprecatory attitude toward himself and his poetry. In short, Kooser's major limitation is a deep-set conservatism that keeps him working in areas he knows he can master to please his audience.

Significantly, however, Kooser's limitations derive directly from his strengths. His narrow technical range reflects his insistence on perfecting the forms he uses. If Kooser has concentrated on a few types of poems, he has made each of these forms unmistakably his own. If he has avoided longer forms, what member of his generation has written so many unforgettable short poems? If he has not cultivated complexity in his work, he has also developed a highly charged kind of simplicity. What his poems lack in intellectuality they make up for in concrete detail. If he occasionally lapses into sentimentality, it is because he invests his poems with real emotion. Even Kooser's self-deprecatory manner betrays a consistent concern for the communal role of the poet. He will not strike superior poses to bully or impress his audience.

Limitations, however, are not necessarily weaknesses. Having catalogued Kooser's conspicuous limitations, one cannot help noticing that they are more often sins of omission than commission. Discussing them may be an interesting critical exercise, but it is useful only insofar as it sharpens one's understanding of Kooser's particular strengths. It may seem obvious to say, but it is surprising how often some otherwise intelligent critics forget, that a writer is better judged by how successfully he works with the material he includes than by what he omits. Kooser's achievement is in the consummate skill with which he handles the self-imposed limits of the short imagistic poem, the universal significance he projects from his local subject matter.

If Kooser's particular achievements as a poet don't fit comfortably into current critical standards, how then is one to judge the extent of the achievement? Here I would submit four simple criteria. After reading carefully through Kooser's work, one should consider the following questions. First, there is the question of quality. Has the author written any perfect poems, not just good poems but perfect ones – on whatever subject, in whatever style, of whatever length – which use the resources of the language so definitively that one cannot change a single phrase without diminishing the poem's effect? And if there are perfect poems, how many? Second, there is the question of originality. Are the author's best poems different from those of any preceding poet? Can one hear a distinctive personality or sensibility behind them that is either saying something new about the world or speaking in such an original way that it makes one see familiar parts of the world as if for the first time? Third, there is a question of scope. How many things can an author do well in his poetry? How many styles or subjects, moods or voices can he master? Fourth, and finally, there is the question of integrity. Do the author's poems hold together to provide a unique and truthful vision of the world, or do they remain isolated moments of illumination?

There are other criteria one might use, but, at the very least, this test helps distinguish a superb poet from one who is merely good. And it is a test that highlights some important ways in which Kooser surpasses some of his more highly praised contemporaries. Kooser has written more perfect poems than any poet of his generation. In a quiet way, he is also one of its most original poets. His technical and intellectual interest may be narrow (indeed, in terms of limited techniques, he shares a common fault of his generation), but his work shows an impressive emotional range always handled in a distinctively personal way. Finally, his work does coalesce into an impressive whole. Read individually, his poems sparkle with insight. Read together, they provide a broad and believable portrait of contemporary America.

2. Popular Poetry And Regional Identity

> All events and experiences are local, somewhere.
> – William Stafford

Popular poets always reflect the general taste and values of a particular time and place, even when those values are at odds with the high culture of the age. Robert Burns's folkish simplicity stands in sharp contrast to the cosmopolitan polish of his eighteenth-century contemporaries, just as Kipling's dance-hall exuberance sounds jarringly unlike the subtle orchestrations of the fin-de-siècle versifiers around him. Popular poetry draws its distinguishing vitality from the particular milieu it shares with its audience. It presents a more relevant world to this constituency than do the traditional topoi of high culture. Rooted in specifics ignored or excluded from mainstream culture, popular poetry therefore often assumes a regional identity. It represents the values and aspirations of a body culturally, politically, and often geographically separate from the ruling class of a nation.

Not surprisingly, therefore, Kooser's popular sensibility expresses itself most clearly in its regional loyalties. Kooser writes about the countryside, weather, towns, and people of the Great Plains. His regional perspective determines not only the subject matter of his poetry but also its texture and thematics. His language, imagery, ideas, attitudes, even his characteristic range of emotions reflect the landscapes, climate, and culture in which he has spent his entire life. To many critics such regionalism still equals provincialism, especially when the region in question is the Middle West. As it also becomes apparent that his work deals more with prosaic small towns and agricultural countryside than the conventionally poetic urban or natural landscapes, his parochialism simply becomes too much for most critics to bear.

Regionalism is ultimately a political term, a dismissive label applied to literature produced in and concerned with areas outside the dominant cultural and economic centers of a society. Classifying a work as "regional" implies that it cannot be judged by "national" standards. It suggests that certain subjects will be of only local interest. Where there are politics, however, there are also coups and revolutions. Sometimes a type of regional writing attains prominence because a new regime has come into power in the literary capital. The rising reputation of Southern literature in America, for example, neatly matches the influx of Southern writers and critics in the late forties into New York and the Ivy League universities.

In most industrialized countries there is also a pervasive urban bias against agricultural areas. In America that prejudice is focused on the Midwest, especially the Great Plains states, which are seen as flat, characterless, and provincial. Unlike the South, an older rural society that defiantly clings to its traditions, or the Southwest, which boasts a continuity of Spanish and Indian culture that has remained relatively intact amid its recent development, the Great Plains was settled later than most other areas of the country. Its economy is also less diversified, its population more widely scattered, and its people less ethnically heterogeneous, consisting largely of assimilated Northern Europeans (Kooser is of German descent). To the outsider there is less obvious local color – no accents, no dramatic social problems, less various scenery – although ironically it is this same uniformity that gives the Great Plains a distinctive cultural identity.

One would think that after Yeats and Faulkner, Joyce and Svevo, Verga and Cather, Cavafy and Hardy, regional writing would no longer be perceived as a second-class artistry practiced by those incapable of presenting the world at large. But although regionalism has become irresistibly attractive as an abstract concept in seminars studying "The Southern Literary Consciousness" or "Poetry and the Irish Revival," it meets with stern resistance when applied to uncanonized regions. The same professor who spent three years researching the facts of Yoknapatawpha County would usually never consider reading a novel by Wright Morris or Leonardo Sciascia. The regionalism celebrated in the universities usually centers on a few familiar territories, which have been described by such a long line of writers that they have been as thoroughly mythologized as Ilium or Rome, rather than the general notion that literature should be rooted in the reality of a particular place. In some cases, like rural Southern fiction or Los Angeles detective writing, one almost wonders if such writing can even still meaningfully be called regional. The local elements have become so thoroughly universalized through continual use that a skillful foreigner might be able to use them convincingly as purely literal patterns. After all, there is a point where the local becomes the universal. Parnassus was once only a small mountain near Delphi and Pan the local deity of impoverished rural Arcadia.

Midwestern critics have not helped the reputation of regional writing. Disenfranchised by a cultural establishment based largely in New York and New England, they have too often lost the objectivity that distance from the literary marketplace should allow. In retaliation to Eastern presumption they have adopted an unconvincing kind of regional boosterism, making extravagant claims for local writers of limited gifts.

While one cannot excuse metropolitan critics for ignoring or undervaluing the work of important regional writers, neither can one sympathize with regional critics for applying looser standards to local writers than to those of national reputation. Regional favoritism is the worst kind of provincialism and eventually undermines the credibility of all local reputations. Here, Midwestern critics could learn from Southerners. While there is no region in America second to the South in the intensity of its literary self-esteem, Southerners have had a long and distinguished tradition of native critics who judged regional writers without losing perspective. Southern critics like Allen Tate, Cleanth Brooks, Robert Penn Warren, Randall Jarrell, John Crowe Ransom, or, more recently, Henry Taylor, George Garrett, Fred Chappell, and William Jay Smith have often discussed their regional writers without lowering their standards.

To some degree, Kooser's reputation has suffered from all of these factors. Rather than viewing his regional roots as a source of authenticity and exactitude, some critics have seen them as parochialism. His local subject matter has been labeled quaint; his affection for the particulars of his native landscape declared sentimental. His insistence on creating a poetic language out of plain Midwestern speech has been construed as a lack of accomplished technique; his deliberate simplicity as folksy ignorance. In short, critics have considered his regional loyalties as limitations. Even more important, however, by labeling Kooser a regional rather than national poet, the majority of critics have missed his grand overriding theme – the gradual disappearance of American rural culture. Focusing on the Great Plains states, Kooser has captured one of the century's great changes, the shift from country to city, from farming to business, from traditional family life to ambiguous personal independence. In hundreds of precise vignettes Kooser has created a poignant mosaic of this cultural transition no less relevant to Abidjan or Osaka than to Omaha or Des Moines. But by stereotyping him as a regional artist, even his admirers have failed to recognize the breadth of his themes. He has been reduced to the product of their expectations.

3. The Development Of A Regional Poet

> A poet's hope: to be
> like some valley cheese,
> local, but prized everywhere.
>
> – W.H. Auden

Ted Kooser's poetic career reveals some of the problems faced by a regional writer who does not either immigrate to a major literary center or join the university network. Born in Ames, Iowa, in 1939, Kooser has spent his entire life in Iowa and Nebraska. He attended Iowa State University, where he majored in English Education. Upon graduating in 1962, he taught high school for a year and then entered a graduate program in English at the University of Nebraska. After one year he stopped full-time study to begin a temporary job in insurance while finishing an M.A. at night. He has worked in insurance ever since and is currently a marketing executive at Lincoln Benefit Life. Thus, Kooser has been doubly alienated from the American literary establishment. First, he has lived only in two agricultural Midwestern states far removed from the centers of literary opinion. Second, he has spent the past twenty-five years working in business, cut off from the academic communities that support most regional writers and provide them with a professional network of colleagues, readers, and reviewers. This isolation would have destroyed most young writers' determination, but in Kooser it nourished an unusually strong sense of independence and self-sufficiency.

Kooser began his publishing career very conventionally, however, with *Official Entry Blank*, his wryly titled first book, which appeared in 1969 as part of the University of Nebraska's short-lived "Poetry from Nebraska" series. Not a precocious volume, *Official Entry Blank* showed a modestly talented young poet trying out a variety of contemporary models as he searched for his own characteristic style. Yet although the volume contained an example of almost every fashionable kind of workshop poem of the period, from heroic couplets to haiku, even those exercises usually gave glimpses of the author's smooth technique and engaging personality. It was an entertaining but curiously unfocused volume, which showed Kooser still writing under the influence of many older poets, most noticeably William Carlos Williams and Karl Shapiro, who had been Kooser's teacher.

Coming upon *Official Entry Blank* in 1969, one would have been hard-pressed either to predict Kooser's subsequent development or to define his individuality as a poet. Reading these poems today, however, one can occasionally hear Kooser's characteristic voice amidst the diversity of borrowed styles. Sometimes humorous, sometimes sober, it is never strained or sarcastic, for Kooser (unlike Whitman and his followers) is a truly democratic poet who addresses the reader as an equal. He never assumes the pose of prophet or professor instructing the unenlightened. He is intimate without being private, never obscure but also never public.

He speaks as one would to an old friend. This tone of quiet trust, which characterizes Kooser's best poetry, may explain why the poet claims to dislike reading his work in public. His poems, he has commented, belong "on a page, not in an auditorium." Conceived in solitude, his poems are best encountered without the theatrical distractions of a public performance.

In *Official Entry Blank* one also notices Kooser's sharp eye for images. Again and again, he catches some tiny detail from everyday life that masterfully evokes a larger scene. He does not yet know how to frame these details for their full effect, but his observations often give these early poems, whatever their faults, an arresting freshness and immediacy. And in a few instances, like "Abandoned Farmhouse," he casts them in a form that foreshadows the best of his later work.

Official Entry Blank was the only immature or derivative book Kooser ever published, but, ironically, it was also the only one for the next eleven years with a university imprimatur. After its publication Kooser disappeared into the gulag of small regional presses. Printed in tiny editions, his books and pamphlets cultivated a small local audience – for some titles probably not more than a few dozen readers. Unnoticed in New York and Boston, they were sometimes reviewed by small and often ephemeral regional magazines like *Great Lakes Review, Raccoon*, and *Dacotah Territory*. More often they were not reviewed at all. But slowly Kooser's reputation grew in the Plains states, though readers and critics elsewhere were not generally aware of his work until the publication of his new and selected poems, *Sure Signs*, in 1980.

Two years after *Official Entry Blank*, Kooser issued a tiny pamphlet with his own illustrations. Self-published by his newly created Windflower Press, *Grass County* announced its intentions to combine "the author's illustrations with his poems in an attempt to more completely convey that vision of the Great Plains introduced in *Official Entry Blank*." Those readers with eyesight sharp enough to decipher its microscopic typeface would have found that the pamphlet actually lived up to its blurb. In *Grass County*'s eight short poems Kooser had found the proper subject and form for his poetry. Here, for example, is "Tom Ball's Barn":

> The loan that built the barn
> just wasn't big enough
> to buy the paint, so the barn
> went bare and fell apart
> at the mortgaged end of twelve
> nail-popping, splintering winters.

> Besides the Januaries,
> the barber says it was
> five-and-a-half percent,
> three dry years, seven wet
> and two indifferent,
> the banker (dead five years)
> and the bank (still open
> but deaf, or *deef* as it were), and
> poor iron in the nails that
> were all to blame for the barn's collapse
> on everything he owned, thus
> leading poor Tom's good health
> to diabetes and
> the swollen leg that threw him
> off the silo, probably
> dead (the doctor said)
> before he hit that board pile.

No single element in "Tom Ball's Barn" is new to American poetry, and yet the combination of these elements strikes a unique note. Without breaking from the past, Kooser had developed a new and personal way to describe the world of the Great Plains, especially the undramatic but tragic lives of its rural people. He had also found a way of universalizing its landscape and stories without losing their local character. He managed ordinary spoken language without making it sound dull and undistinguished.

"Tom Ball's Barn" has another importance in Kooser's career. It is the earliest successful example of the character poem – a kind of poem that would subsequently account for much of his best work. The model for Kooser's character studies were obviously Edwin Arlington Robinson's *Tilbury Town* portraits and Edgar Lee Masters's *Spoon River Anthology* – which remain the two touchstones of American regional poetry – but, as "Tom Ball's Barn" demonstrates, he handled his material very differently. Kooser's portraits have a relentless linearity in their exposition, which endows them with their peculiar speed and powerfully dramatic simplicity. This linearity, however, is balanced by the typically laconic and indirect presentation of the central character.

Syntax is the key to Kooser's expositions. Written in one long sentence, "Tom Ball's Barn" moves quickly through a series of simple observations that the reader immediately understands but has no time to assimilate before his attention is pushed ahead to the next fact. This speed also gives each fact a certain inevitability, as if mere sequence were logic, so that at first glance the callous "thus" in line 17 really does seem to explain Ball's death. Likewise, the reader is immersed in the narrative situation so quickly that he has no time at first to notice the unusual way Ball's story is told. The poem is almost over before Ball is introduced. He is not shown directly; rather he is characterized by the things around him, especially the unpainted barn, whose decay and eventual collapse mirror his own fatal fall. Seen here explicitly for the first time, this equation between people and their property will become a major preoccupation of Kooser's poetry.

That Kooser was unaware of the possibilities he had uncovered in *Grass County* is evident from his next collection, *Twenty Poems* (Best Cellar Press, 1973). This pamphlet shows Kooser uncertain of his direction. While in a few poems, especially the character sketches like "The Failed Suicide" and "Selecting a Reader" (a charming portrait of an ideal reader, who is sensible enough to reject him), Kooser develops the methods he had discovered in *Grass County*, most of the new poems are facile exercises in conventional styles. Here Kooser sometimes explores his characteristic themes but in ways that dilute their effectiveness. There is also a series of macabre poems that matter-of-factly describe weird events – "Grating a Brain," "They Had Torn Off My Face at the Office," and "A Dead Man Driving a Car." Superficially effective, these poems trivialize Kooser's real talent. By affecting the blase tone, the placeless setting, the surreal methods of San Francisco and New York poets, he lost the compassionate authenticity that characterizes his most vital work.

This lack of direction did not last long. The next year Kooser consolidated his achievement in *A Local Habitation & A Name* (Solo Press, 1974). Here, for the first time, he revealed the full range of his talent. Collecting about two dozen of his favorite earlier poems, he added fifty new pieces, including half a dozen perfect poems of unmistakable originality. This volume proved that the intermittent successes of his earlier books had been no fluke. Ranging in tone from comic to tragic, from gently nostalgic to savagely satiric, these new poems, which include such signature pieces as "Spring Plowing," "The Widow Lester," "The Blind Always Come as Such a Surprise," and "A Place in Kansas," showed Kooser capable of handling diverse material in a masterfully personal way. His mastery, however, was of a consciously modest variety. He had chosen the short poem as his medium. All of his poems were shorter than a page, most of them under ten lines. Seen together in bulk for the first time, however, they went beyond a series of dazzling miniatures and formed a memorable composite. All drawing their inspiration from the world of the Great Plains, they re-created that world as effectively in verse as any American poet had done before. Few people on either coast were paying attention (except the maverick William Cole, who in his chatty column in the *Saturday Review* called Kooser his "favorite young poet"), but the Great Plains had just produced a poet of national importance. To show how far Kooser had developed in a few years, one need only compare two short poems that use similar material. First, here is "Haiku for Nebraskans" from *Official Entry Blank*:

> Telephone wires whine
> in the claws of red-tailed hawks –
> frightened mice screaming

In only seventeen syllables, this piece displays many of the conventions of the sixties' workshop poem. Technically competent but uninteresting, it is written in a notoriously easy foreign form that announces its fashionable independence from traditional English metrics. Having been scrupulously compressed to the point of small ellipses, the language is sharp but lackluster. The situation is conveyed visually, the structure of the poem being merely an equation between two images. The content is as unsurprising as the style. The poem begins with an easy contrast between nature and technology (though the technology has been animated - "whining" as it does). Although the ending pretends to be tough and elemental, it is actually cryptically sentimental. Although this poem is skillfully constructed, it ultimately shows no particular virtues to distinguish it from the work of a hundred other poets. Nor does Kooser use his tired images in any way that makes the reader see them with fresh eyes.

Now read "Spring Plowing" from *A Local Habitation & A Name*:

> West of Omaha the freshly plowed fields
> steam in the night like lakes.
> The smell of the earth floods over the roads.
> The field mice are moving their nests
> to the higher ground of fence rows,
> the old among them crying out to the owls
> to take them all. The paths in the grass
> are loud with the squeak of their carts.
> They keep their lanterns covered.

This perfect little poem has no exact precedent in American literature. Deceptively simple on first hearing, it bears sustained attention, and is ultimately satisfying on either a purely naturalistic or imaginative level. Not only is it more technically skilled than the earlier haiku (in the naturalness of the language, the complexity and originality of the imagery, and the structure of its development), but, more important, this poem opens the reader's eyes to the world – albeit some tiny part of a specifically Midwestern world. It enlarges our humanity in ways the earlier poem did not. It will be difficult to drive by a freshly plowed field without thinking of the vulnerable creatures it displaced.

The expository structure of "Spring Plowing" also shows how expert Kooser had become since *Official Entry Blank*. The poem's unexpected movement from ordinary observation to compassionate illumination illustrates Kooser's special achievement as a poet who can endow everyday subjects with a fresh and mysterious resonance. "Spring Plowing" begins conventionally with a description any competent poet might have written, but the first five lines don't prepare one for what will follow. As the poet adjusts his focus from an overview of the field to a close-up of the mice, the scene is suddenly transformed from a naturalistic description to a fantastic, humanized vision of the fleeing animals. Kooser compresses several implicit metaphors into the next four lines, and then ends with a sinister, enigmatic image. The language is highly charged but never clumsy or crowded. The metaphorical trick of transforming mice into threatened refugees is fresh and surprising. Only nine lines long, this poem accomplishes a complex but seamlessly executed shape.

Kooser's next book, *Not Coming to Be Barked At* (Pentagram Press, 1976), solidified his reputation as an important regional poet. (The strange title of this book comes from an incident in the Finnish national epic, the Kalevala, but it is also a typically self-deprecating Kooserian gesture to the reader.) By now Kooser was fully conscious – even if his critics were not – of the position he had created for himself in American poetry as the master of the short, colloquial, imagistic poem. Having perfected his technique, he began broadening his thematics, exploring more fully the world of the Great Plains. *Not Coming to Be Barked At* not only contained many of Kooser's best poems, such as "The Very Old," "Late February," "In a Country Cemetery," "Visiting Mountains," "So This Is Nebraska," and "Shooting a Farmhouse," it also demonstrated the consistent high quality that distinguishes his work. Virtually every poem has some particular virtue to recommend it, and page after page in poems like "Snowfence," "The Afterlife," "North of Alliance," "Old

Soldier's Home," "Sitting All Alone in the Kitchen," "Living Near the Rehabilitation House," and many others, the reader feels the presence of a rich, naturally poetic imagination.

The individual poems were short, but cumulatively they created a powerful picture of a real life in a particular time and place. In his best poetry up to this time Kooser usually maintained a certain distance between himself and his subject. Most often he acted the part of a seemingly impartial observer who stamped his personality on the situation indirectly by choosing the details that he presented or omitted. Sometimes in more openly personal poems he put himself in the action of the poem, but he balanced his direct involvement by deliberately understating the emotional elements of the situation. In *Old Marriage and New* (Cold Mountain Press, 1978), Kooser tried to develop a more openly autobiographical kind of poetry. Writing about the failure of his first marriage and the promise of his second, he carefully established a series of thirteen short scenes that dramatized this difficult period in his life. Sharp and concisely written, these poems seem thin compared to Kooser's previous work. The final twist, with the kind of unexpected image that enlivened so many of his poems, often struck a flat or overly sentimental note here, as in "Driving to Work":

> Once in a while, when I'm driving to work
> in the morning, I see a schoolgirl
> walking slowly along, and something about her
> is you, and the way you must have been
> when you were a girl, still young
> and full of dreams; and seeing you there, oblivious
> to me, I feel as if
> a bird had darted out and struck the windshield.

This poem does not reveal a failure of technique but of sensibility. The final image is too embarrassingly obvious in its appeal to the emotions. One can understand Kooser's pain but cannot share it. *Old Marriage and New* was perhaps a necessary experiment for Kooser, but this chapbook ranks as the weakest of his mature collections.

Kooser remained little known outside the Midwest and under-valued even there until the publication of *Sure Signs: New and Selected Poems* from the University of Pittsburgh Press in 1980. His early career had been sustained by small regional presses and reviews that praised his work but did not distinguish it from that of dozens of other young Plains poets.

Sure Signs not only brought Kooser national attention for the first time. It also established him as one of the few openly regional young poets whose work had broad appeal beyond the Midwest.

Sure Signs showed Kooser as a shrewd judge of his own poetry. He ruthlessly cut away his weaker work and presented the reader with only eighty-nine short poems from all of his earlier books. The careful editing gave *Sure Signs* a consistent quality that put most contemporary collections to shame. It also ensured that readers who came upon Kooser's work there for the first time were left impressed with the quality of his achievement. *Sure Signs* confirmed the poet's peculiar organization of his own work. Kooser has always resisted chronological arrangement of his poems. Instead he has done his best to disguise his own development as a poet by organizing his work in sequences that presumably heighten the particular strengths and variety of his poetry. One can assume from this choice that Kooser, with his characteristic modesty, finds the subjects and moods of his poems more interesting than their evidence of his personal development as a poet. One cannot dispute that decision, but it is important to note here how difficult it makes understanding his development, a difficulty intensified by his insistence on dropping unsuccessful poems from his canon. Only two poems in his confessional book, *Old Marriage and New*, for example, survive in *Sure Signs*.

Based on his first seven books and the considerable number of poems he has published in periodicals since *Sure Signs*, however, it seems appropriate now to attempt some overall conclusions about Kooser's development as a poet. In one way the achronological arrangement of *Sure Signs* testifies to Kooser's lack of dramatic growth. Once he discovered a mature personal voice in *Grass County*, Kooser has demonstrated little substantial change. Although he has experimented with other styles such as the confessional or surreal, these experiments have not generally been successful, and he has returned to a few characteristic kinds of poems. On the other hand, while Kooser's poetry has not greatly changed since *Grass County*, it has deepened. In poem after poem he has gradually populated a region of the imagination, a loving re-creation of the Great Plains. As he has become increasingly conscious of his role in chronicling this region, so much of which is disappearing into history, his work has developed an intensity and integrity few of his contemporaries can match. He has slowly created a larger structure in which his short poems have acquired a new resonance. This regional allegiance has also helped unify his work, focusing the isolated brilliance of his individual poems into one overall vision. Therefore, without abandoning the short forms he has so carefully mastered, Kooser, through the consistency and authenticity of his concerns, has forged them into an ambitious larger work, a unified oeuvre that like an epic encompasses his world.

If Kooser's poetry has grown deeper with each book, it has also grown stronger. Unlike the writing of so many established poets entering middle age, his verse has suffered no drop-off in intensity or workmanship. Experience has only sharpened his skills. Moreover, in developing the overall vision of his work he has never sacrificed the quality and integrity of individual poems to the demands of the larger design. He has not sought refuge in grandiose imaginative schemes but has remained committed to realizing each poem fully in itself, for instinctively he knows that it is not the size of a poet's intentions that ensures survival but the quality of his individual poems. Whatever his other limitations, Kooser has succeeded in the poet's main task – bringing all the forces of language to bear in perfectly achieved poems. Few of his contemporaries have succeeded as often, and none of them in so accessible and engagingly humane a manner. Kooser is unsurpassed in articulating the subtle and complex sensibility of the common American.

Therefore, while one would not claim that Kooser is a major poet, one could well make the case that he will be an enduring one. His work is the genuine article – poetry concerned with themes of permanent value, written flawlessly in an original and distinctive way. However tightly one may draw the boundaries of his accomplishments, once one crosses the border into the territory of his imagination, one finds an unforgettable world of illumination and delight.

BENJAMIN GOTSCHALL ℰᴏ

Benjamin Gotschall grew up on a cattle ranch and dairy in the Sand-hills of Holt County, Nebraska. He earned a degree in English from Nebraska Wesleyan University and a Master of Fine Arts degree from the University of Idaho. He is the author of *Where It Happened* (Sandhills Press, 2008). His work has appeared in *Best New Poets 2007*, *Cadence of Hooves: A Celebration of Horses*, *Meridian*, *Nimrod*, *South Dakota Review*, *Cimarron Review*, *Poetry Southeast*, and *The Meadow*. He is currently a Sandhills rancher and proud pipeline fighter.

These selections come from *Where It Happened*.

ℰᴏ

AT THE AUTO SHOP

While other kids my age
hear the second bell
of the first period
of Monday morning classes
at West Holt High School,
Mom drops me off
on the east side of the shop.

I did my lessons last night
at home, watched the videos that come
every two weeks from Pensacola,
memorized by rote the preamble
to the Constitution, *We the People of the United States*,
fell asleep on my notebook in a puddle
of drool blurring the blue ruling, and woke up

from a dream as I was about to form
a more perfect union with the redhead in the centerfold

of the *Playboy* next to the can
at the auto shop.
After securing her blessings of liberty,
she told me to *Wake up,*
Wake up, in a voice that became my mother's
from the top of the stairs,
stirring me in the sweaty sheets
of my basement bed.

At the auto shop,
Don tells me Lacey Haversham
left her school car in for service,
so with one hand I grasp
a 9/16" wrench, with the other
a keychain bearing the letters L, O, V and E
on each leaf of a green plastic clover.
I think I love Lacey.

I don't know why. Perhaps
the way her first name evokes the mystery
of women's undergarments, or the rhythm
of her second name – *Haversham* –
the emphasis on the first syllable,
reminding me that I want to have her,
and that I don't,
because I can't,
or that I haven't yet,
as I haven't yet kissed a girl
or even held hands.

Neither have I tasted beer, but I smell
its stale sourness on stained floor mats;
nor tried cigarettes, their dusty smoke
emanating from seat fabric
as I park Lacey's car in the shop,
where I promote its general welfare,
take out the radiator to fix the leak,
change the oil filter, check fluids,
belts and hoses. I replace worn brake pads
to provide for the common defense.

To insure domestic tranquility
between Lacey and her dad,
I vacuum ashtrays, spray the dash
with Armor-All, and wash what might be vomit
off the window and the inside of the door,
wondering the whole while
where the party was, if she went
with one of the older boys
or with her girlfriends.

When Lacey arrives for her car, she opens the office door,
smiles, and holds out her hand for the keys,
and as my black-nailed, knuckle-bruised,
grease-stained, calloused fingers drop them into it, I feel
the brief brush of her palm, so soft,
pink and warm it seems
like it couldn't be that clean.

CALF ROPER

My younger brother Marcus backs
his sorrel calf horse Droopy into the box, and stands
in the stirrups, piggin string between his teeth. He leans
over the pommel, and takes a couple practice swings.
Every muscle in the horse's neck is flexed,
veins bulging and ready to explode,
every fibril quivering with pause,
bloodshot eyes unblinking as he waits

for the boot-heel tap that comes
after my brother nods like a surgeon
before the first incision.
This look I have seen
in the practice pen, right before
he lays back the barrier and tracks one down
if he has to, a look I have seen
just before he two-swings the loop,
sticks a fat knot smack on top
of the calf's head with the slack dismounts,
which he does now – left hand sliding rope,

legs pumping in the arena sand – as the horse
sits and the calf hits the end, flips
and gets up winded. Marcus flanks him
easy as folding up a chair, straddles,
strings, two-wraps and a half-hitch
tight, hands in the air
before the dust clears.

Droopy works rope, keeping back
like he's getting paid. Marcus gathers
the jerk-line, hurries calm
back to the horse, mounts slow
to wait for the six-second count.
When the judge's flag drops, the announcer shouts
the time, and I know how high
my brother is by the way he rides out,
head cocked back under his black felt hat, that he knows
what he's done. The blisters on his fingers
don't matter, and neither do bruises

on my feet and legs from pushing calves for him.
I've forgotten hours on the road
burning diesel, listening to the same songs
on the radio, and it's worth
greasy cook-shack burgers and long nights
in the tent under hard rain,

because Marcus and I are drunk
on the silence precision and speed,
and the cries of the cowgirls in the bleachers
who might love my brother as much as I do,
make me understand for a moment
why he's a calf roper, why I
like to watch him
like it's me out there –
doing *just so* and *'cause I can*
doing it
just like that.

CHERRIES

It's what the senior football players call girls
who haven't done it yet, naming them
after what the senior guys are after –
to get one for the first time, before
anybody else, to brag
behind locker room walls
as if it were something to pin
to a letter jacket or dangle
from a rear-view mirror.

I sit in a towel, my feet hot
on cool tile, and listen to Rusty Miller brag
about what he did after the game Friday night:
Lacey Haversham, whose fifteen-freckled nose
and green eyes I long for every day fourth period –
Lacey, who, by sharing a lab tray, makes me
a better biologist. For her
I would dissect a dozen dead frogs
just so she wouldn't have to touch
even one.

I wonder if she felt she had to touch Rusty
in the bench seat of his Chevy. I wonder
if the older cheerleaders told her
what he would be like, that he would tell
the whole football team
the color of her panties,
the noises she made,
how she felt, that he wouldn't kick her out
of bed for eating crackers.

Rusty strides out of the shower, jokes
naked with the quarterback and the left tackle, says
Bet you wish your dick's been half the places mine has,
and, drying it off, says something
about a new record, something
about cherries, and I think of summers,

how I picked them for Grandma Betty
in the trees down by the garden:
each one placed in a Blue Bunny ice-
cream bucket, each one baked
into pie, each one savored
on the tongue, their sour-sweet warmth
mingled with cool vanilla
melting at the spoon's edge. I think
of second-period English class,
Odysseus in the land
of the Lotus eaters. No amount of opium
could tempt me from returning
the spoon to my lips, the taste
still on my tongue as I picture Lacey

on the bench seat of Rusty's Chevy,
moonlight, her red-brown hair
and slender body against his
fullback's shoulders, his long
linebacker's arms. I imagine her dressing
while he takes a piss and grabs
another beer, and I wonder
what it would have been like
to have been him then. I wonder
what kind of taste
it would leave in her mouth
if she knew what she was worth
behind locker room walls.

Twyla Hansen ℘

Twyla Hansen's latest book, *Prairie Suite: A Celebration* (Spring Creek Prairie Audubon Center, 2006) is a poem-drawing collaboration with ornithologist Paul Johnsgard. Her book *Potato Soup* (Backwaters Press, 2003), won the 2004 Nebraska Book Awards competition for poetry, and her writing has appeared in a wide variety of publications, including *Prairie Schooner, Crab Orchard Review, Ascent, Crazy Woman Creek: Women Rewrite the American West* (Houghton Mifflin, 2004), *Poets Against the War* (Nation Books, 2003), and *A Contemporary Reader for Creative Writing* (Harcourt Brace, 1994). Her poems were nominated for the Pushcart Prize in 2001 and 2003. Her previous poetry books are *Sanctuary Near Salt Creek* (Lone Willow Press, 2001), *In Our Very Bones* (A Slow Tempo Press, 1997), and *How to Live in the Heartland* (Flatwater Editions, 1992). She was appointed Nebraska State Poet in 2013.

"Kissing Cousins" was included in *The Decade Dance* (1991); the other three poems included here were published in *The PlainSense of Things 2: Eight Poets from Lincoln, Nebraska* (1997).

℘

Kissing Cousins

I don't know what that means—
kissing cousins—nor do I understand

when Dad says with a wink that the
Andersons are related on both sides,

but what I do know is Myron's eyes
the color of uncut alfalfa, the barn-

loft where we tunnel through bales
to hide from kid sister Ladean, how

we play tag for hours in the pent-up
dust released from the fields, while

the rain at first goes unnoticed, then
pattering harder against the shingles,

darkening the sky which was earlier
filled with April light, earlier warmth

replaced now with a stiff breeze,
Ladean's voice muffled, far away,

me cornered near the haychute, a
charge rising through the unfiltered air,

his lips on mine the surge that quickens
even before the first rumble.

JUST BEFORE DAWN

Just before dawn the great blue heron
glides its bony frame into the dusty light,
flapping slow above the russet field,
giant harvester inching through the rows,
its operator my father, perhaps,
pulling an ancient combine
behind an even older John Deere,
thin brown arms propped over its wheel,
his lungs wheezing, wiping his nose
with a rolled-up sleeve.
I can see his seedcap and work denims,
this scene replayed slowly ten thousand times,
following him after dark into the kitchen,
milking and feeding and fixing complete,
at the sink stripped to his boxers and undershirt,
washing with Lava the day's grit off
his leathery face and arms,
aroma of supper and sweat and soap,
his old-fashioned wire-rims and old country

references, hold-over from the last century,
not embarrassing me now –
flying above it all,
settling down onto shallow water,
body erect, senses alert, all alone.

THE OTHER WOMAN

as I picture her
she has no basil
no cumin
no sun-hardened hyssop
nor sage around her eyes

she never catnips
but laughs comfrey
tansy with a primula smile

as I think of her
she's angelica
foxglove and jasmine

somewhat peppermint
not letting you see
all her saffron at once

one day I'll meet her
that rue woman
that wild indigo teasel
somewhere neutral
free of woodruff and of dropwort
some summer savory

she's the nose
set to lavender
eye full of sesame
ear ringing rosemary

she's wind
through wild thyme

THIS EARLY EVENING

This early evening he is on top of plywood
on top of what will be roof of the new addition,
crawling around, nailing down tar paper.

I cannot watch him lean toward the edge
with the round metal disks, hammer, nails.
I don't know why,
               why at heights my legs
stiffen when I must descend, why I suddenly
feel heavy or clumsy or both.

Last year at the Anasazi ruins, tall ladders
taking us from one ancient level to the next.
he laughs at photos – *look, she's got a death grip
on that rung.*
Now's the time for deftness and buoyancy,
sweetness and light. The gravity of air,
not earth, balancing on the tip of a feather.
Think bird and wing, the parting of airwaves.

This early evening from a ladder on the edge
of the new roof, my knees weak, watching him,
and overhead, gulls circling,

               circling and
turning, disappearing over the treetops,
the sun hitting their undersides as if cotton
hankies in the sky, floating,
             soaring,
in early fall a gathering of robust gulls
going south, their webbed feet dangling freely
in the wind, along for the ride.

JONATHAN HOLDEN &

Jonathan Holden, Kansas' first poet laureate, is an English professor and poet-in-residence at Kansas State University. He earned his doctorate degree in 1974 at the University of Colorado in Boulder. His works include *The Old Formalism: Character in Contemporary American Poetry* (1999), *Knowing: New and Selected Poems* (2000), and *Guns and Boyhood in America: Memoir of Growing Up in the '50s* (1997). He has received numerous creative writing awards and two National Endowment for the Arts fellowships.

The poems included here come from *The Decade Dance* (1991).

&

SHOPTALK

> The best talk in the world is professional shoptalk.
> It doesn't matter if it's among stock-car drivers, geometers,
> chefs, cops, or financiers. It's fascinating, even if you
> don't understand a word.
> —observation of a friend

I like this low, comfortable kind
of conversation which the rain's
been having with itself all day
as it goes about its business,
deftly assembling its tiny parts,
confident, in no great hurry,
discussing, perhaps, the different
gutters it has seen, the taste of rust
in New York, the rust in Chicago.
Or perhaps comparing notes
about the finer points of roofs,

where best to creep to find
flaws in asphalt shingles,
or maybe it's murmuring in rain-jargon
over different grades of redwood,
the rates they rot. No end of stories
which it could be telling—
the drudgery of cycling in a monsoon,
monotony of equatorial assignments,
the same steamy party each afternoon.
Or maybe the gossip's of some great
typhoon, the melee of another
grand convention. Or is it muttering
about the way some thunderstorms
rig their elections, the social
life of rain in some bayou,
as the rain keeps up its quiet
shoptalk—the level, reassuring
talk of people who are comfortable
again, sure what they're doing,
graceful in their work, and accurate,
serious in the way that rain
is serious, given over to their task
of touching the world.

MIDWAY

Nighthawks turn up like lost cousins
like slippers old men leave under the bed,
erasing the reasons I am here today
in Wilber, Nebraska, looking up at the sky.
Marriage or mirage, the parade is long gone.
I am thirsty for perfection, over thirty,
unlike the majorette in silver sequins
with golden thighs and the Czech King—
a Tony Curtis look-alike from Crete.
The hot street dulls with spit and beer.
I've come with a lover,
that American gypsy we all claim never to forget
though names drift away like chaff.

But corn is high enough in August
to be seen from town, the women playing bingo
while their men crack old jokes behind the hotel.
Polka bands wheeze up and down on flatbeds
between promotions of the lottery
and people talking. A middle-aged couple, red-faced
and sweating, dance without thinking
to Gary Grossova's Chevroletkas—
fathers of the town in black vests, hearts
embroidered on their backs.
A red skirt twirling on a woman
tells time. I am flirting hard
with the airbrush artist from Lincoln, leaning
against his wooden booth to finger candy-colored shirts.
Smells of kraut and jaternice make me dizzy.
In the Foxhole Bar a girl is dancing on a table,
her hair wavering like woodsmoke through the open door,
tempting the old men chewing tobacco
on a makeshift bench in front of Pythian Hall.
They stare awhile before blinking.
Muscle boys from the Omaha Sokol do backflips in time
to tambourines, their butts flashing red satin
like human neon, showing how it's done.
What will it cost me to stop on the midway
and look as long as I want? I watch the guy I want
airbrush hearts, charting the course of air
as it turns color, fluorescing shirts like souls.
Children and the crippled stay the longest
just to see how rainbows happen without the flood
before they are sold. The light is in our eyes
when the clown floats past playing accordian—
some song we know, but we stop and listen anyway
unable to help ourselves.

WILLIAM KLOEFKORN 🖎

William Kloefkorn was named the Nebraska State Poet by proclamation of the Unicameral in 1982. A long-time professor of English
at Nebraska Wesleyan University in Lincoln, he authored many collections of poetry and other books, including *Alvin Turner as Farmer* (Logan
House, 2004), *Sunrise, Dayglow, Sunset, Moon* (Talking River Publications,
2004), and *Walking the Campus* (Lone Willow Press, 2004). He has also
published four memoirs, *This Death by Drowning* (U of Nebraska P, 2001),
Restoring the Burnt Child (U of Nebraska Press, 2003), *At Home on This
Moveable Earth* (U of Nebraska Press, 2006), and *Breathing in the Fullness of
Time* (U of Nebraska P, 2009). His introductory statement was written in
2009. He died in 2011.

"The Feedlot Buffalo" was published in *The Sandhills & Other Ge-
ographies* (1980); "Walking Lake Leba" and "Shoe" were included in *The
PlainSense of Things 2: Eight Poets from Lincoln, Nebraska* (1997); "Oral
Interpretation," "Shooting the Rabbit," and "Overtime" were included in
Among the Living (1999), a Main-Traveled Roads chapbook.

NOTE FROM KLOEFKORN ABOUT SANDHILLS PRESS

To those who enjoy and appreciate contemporary poetry, the Sandhills Press is a moveable feast—moveable because its editor and publisher, Mark Sanders, is productively mobile. Wherever he goes, the
Sandhills Press goes with him. They are joined not only at the hip, but
likewise at the gut and the neocortex. For thirty years, and more than a
half a dozen locations—mostly colleges and universities—Sanders has
managed to sustain and promote his press, and most often doing it without a single dollar of grant money. When he was teaching at Lewis-Clark
State College in Lewiston, Idaho, for example, he convinced the authori-
ties that the school needed its own press. The upshot was the creation
of Talking River Publications, and I was honored to have been its first
author—a collection of poems titled *Sunrise, Dayglow, Sunset, Moon*.

The press's list of titles and authors is beyond impressive: Kathleene

West, *Plainswoman*; Barton Sutter, *Pine Creek Parish Hall and Other Poems*; Barbara Schmitz, *How to Get Out of the Body*; Mary Kathryn Stillwell, *Moving to Malibu*. And many more, including a number of anthologies. As a small, non-profit press, Sandhills does not publish work that other larger presses refuse to publish; it publishes work that the larger presses do not have the common sense, or editors with down-to-earth judgment, to consider. Most recently the Sandhills Press (now operating in Nacogdoches, Texas) published Ben Gotschall's first book of poetry, *Where It Happened*, one of the strongest collections that I have read in a long, long time.

Commitment. Perseverance. Respect for the written word. This triad has kept the Sandhills Press alive for three decades, and today, in spite of occasional setbacks, it continues to flourish. It has a regional focus, but many of the poems probe and enlighten subjects and themes that are common to everyone, making "small" and "non-profit" relative, if not outright irrelevant, designations.

℘

THE FEEDLOT BUFFALO

(for Stan Smith)

He can never understand
that in spite of all his heft,
in spite of his curious hump,
in spite of those two unbalanced weights
that hang like globes ensacked between his legs,
he is token.
He understands himself instead
to be one of the current herd,
which is why,
looking into the eyes of a steer,
he sees himself as brother.
He assumes that all those others gathered here
must likewise feel the weight between their legs,
that deep beneath the shag of memory
they too dream of grazing down
all fences, endlessly.
Yet something is not precisely right,

and he knows it.
Fattened, the steers leave home,
and the feedlot buffalo (until
a young and lean supply
arrives to fill the scene)
is left alone to wonder.
What has gone wrong?
Had he the answer,
the feedlot buffalo
might assume this throne,
might loosen
from his grand and ancient head
the lode of history.

But the question persists, without answer,
while the feedlot buffalo
roams the herd,
displaced, misled, inferior.
However huge,
he will not be singled out
for whatever gift it is
that lies beyond those rows of neck-worn troughs.
More complete than he can ever know,
he looks among the latest tender crop
(himself the most elusive of them all)
for something that he must believe
is missing.

ORAL INTERPRETATION: APRIL, 1945

This year at the regional festival
we draw titles from the deep well
of a judge's hat. Mine: *Abraham Lincoln
Walks at Midnight*.

I read the poem without looking at the text,
read it believing in the power
of eye contact – but
I pronounce *portentous* incorrectly,

and I speak the question that ends the poem
as if it were declarative, a sin
that not even eye contact
has the wherewithal to redeem.

Basso profundo is what the judge calls
my voice, praising its timbre until I beam,
then with hat in hand he notes the transgressions
and scores me down.

When the day for the state competition
rolls around
I throw defeat to the south wind and go
fishing. Just me
and the pond and the hoppers, blue sky
and bunchgrass and crawlers enough
for a lifetime.

Portentous. From the Latin *portentosus,* meaning
ominous or foreboding. Yet the sun
shines brightly and the largemouth are biting.
Yet a cottonwood near the water
casts a reflection only the disenfranchised
can discern: Lincoln under a high
top-hat, his suit black, his face bronzed,
his body lank.

When the sun becomes too much
I head home. *The sins of all the war-lords*
burn his heart. It's pentameter,
meaning a line of verse consisting of five
metrical feet, from the Greek *pente,* five, and
metron, a measure. And

O how the measures sing! *It breaks his heart*
that kings must murder still.... Yet
the largemouth sizzling in the skillet
waters the tongue. Yet tomorrow and tomorrow
can't you hear the sounds of footsteps
echoing on the sidewalk in front of the drugstore
and the pool hall into dawn?

OVERTIME

(for Eloise Ann)

The ball, having kissed the backboard,
falls through the hoop, up-
ending the nylon net,

and my wife with an elbow
cracks another of my ribs – because
mayhem too
can be a form of love
when it arrives on the heels
of justice, Good Guys
victorious, Bad Guys
whipped,

and what I'd like
more than anything
is a chocolate malt
in a drugstore somewhere
in Kansas, just me and the malt
and my girlfriend
sitting in a booth
freezing our lips

and talking about our future,
both of us wanting
more than anything
to be sitting together – our
children and their children
happy and away from home-making
fists at the numbnut officials,
cheering the Good Guys on.

SHOE

I am the shoe I threw away last summer, man,
on the river, man, man floating
in a jonboat in a current of the Loup, man,
man who in a burst of anger
or maybe deep delight
tossed the shoe into the channel, man,
man who thought he'd never see the shoe
again, man, man with one shoe on,
one shoe off, man, O I am the shoe
I threw away last summer, man,
man drifting now wherever
those tides of fortune and misfortune
take me, man, I am that
unable-to-toss-myself-away man, man,
O I am the shoe I threw away last summer, man,
I am the fit, man, the perfect fit, the
go-to-meeting man, man, man wearing himself
in spite of himself, man, heel to toe, man,
toe to heel, man, forward march column left
to the rear, man, man going hey and diddle-diddle
straight up the middle, man, man
in the middle, man, O man, O shoe,
don't let the bastards ever (do you hear me?)
wear you down.

SHOOTING THE RABBIT

Now the dilemma is whether to dig out the old
Red Ryder air rifle, load it with shot
and tiptoe into the backyard,
or let the cottontail
finish its breakfast of hosta and dianthus.

> Grandfather's 12-gauge, after
> an explosion too violent
> ever to be prepared for,
> released an aroma not even

the Fourth of July could
measure up to. It hung
suspended in the cold December air
as if wanting to be taken in. And
I took it in, acrid and sweet.
And the cottontail lay
splayed and amazed
in the fresh white snow.
I resolve the dilemma by waiting, as always,
for my wife to resolve it. With her voice
and a yellow teatowel she spooks the rabbit,
calling it names not at all generic.

We named our first son John,
after my brother, who carries
our other grandfather's name,
grandfather blown away
by indeterminate winds four years
before my brother was born.
Had I shot the rabbit my wife, having many times
entreated me to shoot the rabbit,
would have denounced me for shooting the rabbit.
Isn't there something here worth taking in?

We sit meanwhile on the patio in metal
high-backed chairs that rock. Another burst
of early-morning news
hangs suspended in the mild April air. Air
more acrid than sweet. We rock and rock.
amazed and grateful to be counted yet
among the living.

WALKING LAKE LEBA, EARLY JUNE
(for Don and Gloria)

After the fireworks
a dense effluvium of potassium nitrate
hangs suspended in the thin Colorado air,

and I am in Nebraska walking again the shores of Leba,
walking with friends the narrow gravel road
that under moon and starlight

will take us to the far end of the lake,
will return us then to where we spent
the long liquid edges of the evening

watching pyrotechnics, glitter and glitz, poof and hiss,
boomalay, boomalay, boom! boom! boom! And
because we are too young ever to be older

we break, then break again, the night's sudden stillness
with our audacious laughter. God, we know,
lies in the details: sumac, cottonwood, bur oak,

willow. And the catfish we ate
before we caught it, one good line
deserving another. And the human voice at midnight

palpable as the water we washed away our sins in –
and later, many moons removed from these lofty mountains,
our silences in sleep joining

the everlasting swell of silence.

TED KOOSER ☙

Dana Gioia once stated that Kooser had "written more perfect poems than any poet of his generation." Poet and critic David Baker (also included in this anthology) wrote: "Kooser documents the dignities, habits, and small griefs of daily life, our hunger for connection, our struggle to find balance in natural and unnaturally human worlds." In announcing his appointment as Poet Laureate, Librarian of Congress James Billington said, "Ted Kooser is a major poetic voice for rural and small town America and the first Poet Laureate chosen from the Great Plains. His verse reaches beyond his native region to touch on universal themes in accessible ways."

Kooser has authored numerous collections of poetry, including *Flying at Night* (University of Pittsburgh Press, 2005), *Winter Morning Walks: One Hundred Postcards to Jim Harrison* (2000), which won the 2001 Nebraska Book Award for poetry; *Weather Central* (1994); *One World at a Time* (1985); and *Sure Signs* (1980). His nonfiction books include *The Poetry Home Repair Manual: Practical Advice for Beginning Poets* (University of Nebraska Press, 2005) and *Local Wonders: Seasons in the Bohemian Alps* (University of Nebraska Press, 2002). His many honors include two NEA fellowships in poetry, a Pushcart Prize, the Stanley Kunitz Prize from Columbia, the Boatwright Prize from *Shenandoah*, the Pulitzer Prize for *Delights & Shadows* (Copper Canyon, 2004), and an appointment as U. S. Poet Laureate. He is a professor in the English Department of the University of Nebraska-Lincoln. He lives on an acreage near the village of Garland, Nebraska, with his wife Kathleen Rutledge.

"Beer Bottle" appeared in *The PlainSense of Things: Eight Poets from Lincoln, Nebraska* (1997) and as a Sandhills broadside; "Laundry" appeared in *The Sandhills & Other Geographies* (1980) and as a Sandhills broadside; "Etude" and "The Times of Their Lives" were also included in *The PlainSense of Things 2;* and, "Gold Leaf" and "Riding with Colonel Carter" appeared in the Main-Traveled Roads chapbook, *Riding with Coloner Carter: An Essay and Two Poems* (1999).

NOTE FROM KOOSER ABOUT SANDHILLS PRESS

When I came to Nebraska 46 years ago there were two literary magazines, *Prairie Schooner* at the university, and *Steppenwolf,* an independent journal coming out of Omaha. The University of Nebraska Press was the only publisher of books of poetry. Within a few years, the press discontinued the poetry series, apparently killed off by poor sales of books like my first, *Official Entry Blank* and Don Jones' *Medical Aid and Other Poems.* At the end of the Sixties, Greg Kuzma arrived and began publishing chapbooks and his journal, *Pebble,* and I had begun to publish a journal and collections of poetry under my Windflower imprint. My journal was called *The Salt Creek Reader* and then *The New Salt Creek Reader* and then *The Blue Hotel.* Under the Windflower imprint I published Don Welch's first book, *Dead Horse Table,* and republished Bill Kloefkorn's first, *Alvin Turner as Farmer* and his second, *Uncertain the Final Run to Winter.* By the early Seventies Roy Scheele returned from teaching in Tennessee and he and Adam Staib were publishing a journal, too, called *Tin Roof Blues.* Concurrent with all that activitiy there appeared yet another independent journal, *Saltillo.* Suddenly there were little fires of enthusiasm for writing burning here and there on the prairie.

I think I have all that right, but am probably forgetting some things. What I'd like to emphasize is that there was quite a bit of literary activity, considering we were living in a state with a population of a little over a million. But with the exception of *Prairie Schooner* and The University of Nebraska Press there was no steady and reliable flame until Mark Sanders began his imprint, Sandhills Press. From the first, it seemed to me that Mark had the love of Plains literature and the stubborn perseverance that would make his contribution significant and lasting. And I was right to think so. Sandhills Press has come at readers on the Plains from many directions over the years, always with an engaging manner and artful presentation. Mark's vocation as teacher has taken him in a great and ever widening circle out and around Nebraska but Sandhills' Nebraska origins, somewhere out in the center of our state, have always been the axis, have always been the point where the kite string was tucked under a rock to keep the kite from getting lost on the wind. If we have an axis for our writing, it is Don Welch at Kearney, and Mark was his student. And though the wind has blown hard, Sandhills has survived, and to this day, years and years later, is still making a terrific contribution to Nebraska's and the Great Plains' arts and letters.

BEER BOTTLE

In the burned-
out highway
ditch the throw-

away beer
bottle lands
standing up

unbroken,
like a cat
thrown off

of a roof
to kill it,
landing hard

and dazzled
in the sun,
right side up;

sort of a miracle.

ETUDE

I have been watching a Great Blue Heron
fish in the cattails, easing ahead
with the stealth of a lover composing a letter,
the hungry words looping and blue
as they coil and uncoil, as they kiss and sting.

Let's say that he holds down an everyday job
in an office. His blue shirt blends in.
Long days swim beneath the glass top
of his desk, each one alike. On the lip
of each morning, a bubble trembles.

No one has seen him there, writing a letter

to a woman he loves. His pencil is poised
in the air like the beak of a bird.
He would spear the whole world if he could,
toss it and swallow it live.

LAUNDRY

A pink house trailer,
scuffed and rusted, sunken
in weeds. On the line,

five pale blue workshirts
up to their elbows
in raspberry canes,

a good, clean crew
of pickers, out early,
sleeves wet with dew,

and near them, a pair
of bright yellow panties
urging them on.

GOLD LEAF

The window delivery truck
with its racks of green-edged plate glass
flashing on either side
rolls through the shifting, shimmering colors
of summer, reflecting everything,
present and past,
then stops at a traffic signal,
and in the slanting, glancing light
of more than forty years ago
there I stand, watching my teacher,
the signpainter, letter a window in gold,
rubbing a stick in his hair to build a charge,
then taking the lid from a box
and with his stick so carefully lifting

a shuddering mirror of gold
and placing it over the tacky varnish
of the letter *S*. But before he can finish
even one word from the past,
the present presses in, the light turns green,
and the window truck,
ablaze with other people's memories,
rolls on.

RIDING WITH COLONEL CARTER

I have from time to time been asked about my influences, about the experiences I had when young that were to shape my literary life. If I set aside the Walt Disney animated films, which my poems still resemble, the most important influence was *Lentil*, a children's story written and illustrated by Robert McCloskey. It was first published by The Viking Press in 1940, and my copy was given to me by friends of my family while I was in grade school. In neat but labored cursive I carefully inscribed the title page, "This book belongs to the Library of Teddy Kooser." I was already showing the tell-tale signs of the bibliophile I would one day become.

Lentil is the story of a schoolboy who, by what we in my family called stick-to-it-iveness, overcomes an inability to fit into the life of his community and becomes a local hero. It is no surprise that I identified with the protagonist. He was a boy about my age, ten or twelve; the author's wonderfully detailed pencil drawings of street scenes in the fictional small town of Alta, Ohio, looked much like my home town of Ames, Iowa; and the problem Lentil had in fitting in was a problem I had.

It's a simple story. Lentil occupies himself in the ways I once did, walking around town, up and down alleys, thinking about his place in the world. His main problem is that he is frequently embarrassed in the schoolroom because he is unable to sing as sweetly as his classmates. When he opens his mouth, he croaks. So he saves his pennies, purchases a harmonica, and practices it wherever he goes, hoping that by the sweetness of his harmonica-playing he will be redeemed in the eyes of his classmates.

The villain in the story is an old man named Sneep, the town spoilsport and sourpuss. Sneep doesn't like much of anything, and he especially doesn't like the town's most notable citizen, Colonel Carter. Sneep and Colonel Carter are about the same age, and perhaps Sneep, who has never made much of himself, is jealous of Colonel Carter, who is a wealthy benefactor and noted public servant. When the news gets out that the Colonel is coming back to Alta after two years away, old Sneep determines to spoil the celebration.

The townspeople deck out the town in bunting for the Colonel's arrival, and everybody gathers at the railroad depot to meet his train. A brass band has assembled, prepared to lead a parade through the streets. But Old Sneep gets on top of the depot roof and, when the train comes in, starts loudly slurping on a lemon. As a result, all of the band members pucker up, unable to blow their trumpets and trombones and tubas.

But Lentil is miraculously unaffected by Sneep's dirty trick, and he pulls out his harmonica and begins to play. The Colonel is so pleased with Lentil's music, especially his rendition of "She'll Be Comin' 'Round the Mountain," that he jigs a few steps on the depot platform and then lets Lentil ride with him at the head of the parade in his open touring car. All has gone well. Even Old Sneep is softened up by the music. On the last page of the book is a drawing of Lentil smiling, with the single sentence, "So you never know what can happen when you learn to play the harmonica."

When I was a boy, I felt a lot like Lentil. Surely, the success of a story like his – I believe Lentil went through many reprintings – has to do with the fact that many if not most children feel they don't fit in. At that time I was small and awkward and no good at athletics, the true measure of acceptability in those days. I tried hard. I strapped on the football helmet my parents had lovingly bought me, and got run right over as if I'd been a sandbag somebody had left on the playground. I couldn't run as fast, jump as far or as high, or talk the sports lingo as well as my classmates. I knew I'd never fit in. So I decided I'd have to find something I could do well if I wanted to be loved and admired. Inspired by *Lentil*, I bought a harmonica and tried to learn to play it. It was one of the Hohner "Old Standby" models, and though I practiced a lot, the only tune I ever learned to execute well was "Red River Valley." This modest accomplishment was never going to get me into the big parade.

I was better at drawing pictures and writing poems and stories, and eventually I converted my aspirations to becoming an artist and author. I had teachers who understood how important it is not to discourage children while they play with their crayons and pencils. They didn't tell me that my trees looked too much like lollipops or that my stories didn't end with a proper denouement. They smiled and patted my shoulder and ran their warm fingers through my hair. I know now that I was in the presence of the only angels we are ever likely to make the acquaintance of: teachers blessed with the love of small people who are trying to find their place in the world.

Some years later, when in the summers I worked as a sign painter, I used to drive my old pickup truck into small towns in Iowa that were much like Alta, Ohio, Lentil's town, and set about to letter the glass windows of storefronts on Main Street. Old men would come out of the taverns and coffee shops, carrying folding chairs, and would sit behind me and watch me work. I was that exotic creature, an itinerant artist, and their attention and admiration warmed my back with a kind of bone-deep sunshine. There is nothing so pleasant as to have the admiration of those people we have come to call the locals.

But it was as a poet that I would finally become my own Lentil. Because he was interested in writing and writers, Bob Kerrey, now Nebraska's senior Senator, asked a mutual acquaintance to introduce me to him. This was in the 1970s, before he was to run for governor. He and I became fast friends, beginning an exchange of yarns and letters that continues today. When he was elected governor, Bob would occasionally drive out to our place in the country for a visit. He would dismiss his official driver, a trooper, and would himself pilot the official governor-mobile, a long black Chrysler or Lincoln, I forget which.

Sometimes we'd go for a drive. We'd roll up and down the gravel roads, talking books and telling stories and laughing and raising a great plume of gubernatorial dust, and it came to me that there I was, at last, Lentil, riding in Colonel Carter's car at the head of the parade. You just never know what can happen when you learn to play the harmonica.

THE TIME OF THEIR LIVES

Today my ducks are eating windfalls
under the broken Jonathan tree –
nine white Pekins laughing like nuns
on a picnic, rolling the apples around
in the grass with their orange bills,
having the time of their lives.

Nothing escapes them. Near them,
a red leaf rides the long grass

with a papery rattle. A sweat-bee
deep in an apple sucks
the tart cider. A lacy elm leaf
sifts the wind. Their black eyes sparkle.

There is already ice in the reeds
at the edge of the pond. I have built
a cage in the dark garage, for tomorrow
they go to a hard young farm wife
easy with killing. They will be
packaged like gifts, heavy as hearts.

Their cage is sturdy, quick to close.
As my hammer tapped, they arched their necks
to hear better the tick of scales
as a bull snake passed. Above the cry
of my table saw, they heard a hawk's wings
dust the blue bowl of the sky.

GREG KOSMICKI ℰↄ

Greg Kosmicki is the founder and publisher of The Backwaters Press. He is the author of numerous books of poems and chapbooks. He has been awarded an Individual Artist Fellowship twice by the Nebraska Arts Council. Garrison Keillor has read his poems on Writers' Almanac.

"What I Like" and "My Flag" appeared in *We have always been coming to this morning* (2007). "West of Grand Island," "The Possum," "I wanted to draw a picture of my son," "Add to That List," "The Three-Minute Egg," "My Flat," and "What I Like" were taken from the Main-Travelled Roads Chapbooks, *For My Son In a Motel Room*, and *tables, chairs, wall, window*.

NOTE FROM KOSMICKI ABOUT SANDHILLS PRESS

Like some mythological king condemned by an inscrutable brutal god to wander the barrens because he loved his country too much, Mark Sanders has roamed from teaching post to pillar throughout the American Midwest, the southwest, and the west, always alone, always at odds with any no-place he came to rest that was not home. Wherever he travelled he kept his native skies locked in his heart, the swell of the grasslands in his sight—a pilgrim carrying his keepsake box of the old sod in the locker of his soul. Out of the depths of this love of the land and the language it engendered in him, he fathered and birthed Sandhills Press, a true lovechild if ever there was one, nursed it alive, and fathered it through the cataclysms of his life, through the dark hours, the wrenching sadnesses, through all the terrors that he came to know as his daily fare.

The poets of Nebraska, the poets of the Midwest, the poets of the world need to stand up for a hero's welcome the day that Mark Sanders walks back into his home state, not broken, but free— for here is a man who has kept alive the words, who words have kept alive.

ℰↃ

West of Grand Island

We are driving towards sunset through sky peppered with geese
that are always there, but you just can't see,
you can't see them until you move through time, and space,
through air, through some life, to the place
where they poke through,
pinpricks of dark light on the purple-orange crazy
of sunset, then there they are, and you know
this is another miracle you are witnessing, sure as dawn
sure as sunset, sure as hurtling through space on the planet
hurtling through space, sure as your mother rose up
one day to lie down to press you out from
between her thighs, her love, sure as where you see them then
spread obscenely before you hours later where she lies
in the hospital recovering poorly from surgery, unaware she is there,
unaware you are there because she is ill, in her mind,
unaware these geese had landed in this small puddle
outside Grand Island, that you and your wife
and her granddaughters had seen them as they drove through time
disguised as air, seen them, as if on a signal, rise, ten thousand wings
raising dark bodies out of black water, into the waning light.

The Possum

I was talking on the phone the other night
to this guy about some peace stuff
when this possum ran through the light
in the back yard as I looked
out the window. I yelled to Debbie
and Audrey to come quick.
I really wanted to hang up
but I couldn't because we
were right in the middle of a conversation
about the annual State peace conference
two days away, and he had

some stuff he wanted to clear up
about a survey. So we talked
and Debbie and Audrey looked out
the window, and Audrey said
Yech! It's so ugly!
She wanted to go outside
and stamp on the deck to scare it.
I covered the phone and said
Leave it alone! It has enough
to deal with in its life!
I was sort of thinking about
my mother too. She's been locked up
the last few days in a mental ward
because her dementia spun out of control
after some surgery. My dad
didn't know what else to do.
She refused to go in the rest home.
The one in their town
wouldn't take her. So they drove her
over to Scottsbluff and Dad
had her committed. Everybody
felt terrible. Mom
most of all. She had cried to me
on the phone the night before
that her life was over
that she was just stuck in there to die.
She thinks everybody's plotting against her –
who wouldn't? So I'm talking to this guy,
Debbie and Audrey are looking out the window,
they're excited. You don't get to see
a possum every day. Then Audrey
went outside to scare it away
but it was already heading toward the trees
at the back of the yard.
When I saw it, the possum had run
right through the pool of light
just like it was unaware how exposed it was.
Ran right through there
and seemed to stay, caught in my vision,
triangular white face, black beady eyes,

stay there in that flood of light.
But it was moving, all along
and the guy and I were talking
on the phone, and my mother
was sleeping, I hope, in her bed
on the mental ward. A bed
made cold by despair, a bed
she could not run away from
into the dark, where the trees are,
the deep wilderness at the end of our lives.

MY FLAG

It is after dinner and I go to shake
the crumbs from the tablecloth.
They fall down onto the porch steps

for the crickets and the mice and ants.
We live in a great country,
there is enough for all.

The tablecloth unfurls lightly on the held breath
of the still fall night air
and it seems to me to be like a flag

with the blue stripe all around the border
and the blue stripe enclosing the field at center,
a field that encloses some flowers

but could not hold in even all the flowers
since some of them have escaped
and drifted, as on water or a breeze

toward the bright blue border.
It is the flag of the friendly country,
where even the vermin have enough to eat,

and I'm waving it from my porch for everyone.
I want you to come and join me
and my family, I want you to sit

at my table and have bread and lasagna with us
so we can talk about the war and the taxes,
I want you to help me shake crumbs on the porch,

I want to wash it and iron it and fold it safely,
to place it gently and with respect in the drawer
for our next dinner when we will not have

marched under any other flag
for I know you could not be a traitor to me.
We will all be so insanely happy

we had not yet had to die for any cause.
I want you to spill your wine.
I want you to get bread crumbs on my flag.

WHAT I LIKE

is when the lights are out in the house and I'm heading off to bed in
my sock feet and I step on one of the boards in the floor and it gives

a little. What I like is when I get a letter from somebody and can
tell the person who sent it to me is a smoker because the envelope

and the letter smell like stale smoke. What I like is to get some
honey on my fingers, just a little bit, and not know it and get

it on something else like a knife handle or a doorknob, and then have
to try and figure out all the places I got honeyed up. And what I

like is to run some warm water on a white dishrag and go around
and wipe all the honey off all the things I got the honey on. And what

I like too is to open a new book and put it up to my face and flip
the pages to smell the ink and paper smell come out of the book.

And I like to check a book out of a library and find a cigarette
ash in it or a crumb of something or a piece of snot. Maybe

you are the one who left it there. I like to know that
there are others living here, doing the same things I am doing.

I like to be in traffic, maybe right behind your truck,
and smell the tinny stench of your exhaust. I like to know

you are on your way, and that I am following along behind
or maybe even am headed on my way too. I like to know that

people are headed on their ways, even if they don't know where they
are going. I like to be part of that. Even though it makes me

almost blow chunks, I like to smell your bad breath because
you are alive, and you are talking to me. Oh sure, I like

to smell the hyacinths in the grocery store
somebody broke off that hang there like,

well, broken hyacinths.
What I like is that even someone's destructive urge

or some dumb accident
can't stop us from knowing we are alive.

I WANTED TO DRAW A PICTURE OF MY SON

sleeping on the floor on his pillow
but he is so beautiful I can't do it
maybe if he were ugly I could
a few warts here and there
could make it easier
but he is perfect his hair
his skin and the turn of his nose
his perfect ear showing under his new
semi-perfect haircut

the barber doesn't get an "A"
he did pretty good
with his scissors but

not as good as me with
my giant dong and my
wife with her pulsating vagina
still and all it is amazing
how that one unravaged
sperm found its way
the single one I had in me
probably at that time
not damaged by acid or cigarettes
not wrecked by long nights drunk
under the trees and the stars
on cold lawns, or scorched by coffee
not mutilated by football or wars
and chemicals from the grocery store
and the water and the air
and the one perfect egg
she laid that month with
none of her family size
(small) or of either
side's noses (giant)
or ears (even bigger)
and none of the myriad pile
of genetic defects this tiny
family (that of Man and Woman)
inbred into itself
genetic abnormalities
a better chance than not
it is amazing
the single uncrippled
unbroken untwisted undamaged
sperm met with the Blessed
Virgin of all eggs

I can still remember
that hot night
in summer it was
raining or about to
rain or it was
dry and hot or
snowing

I had been working
hard on some new
poetic excrescence
she had been
reading *Penthouse*
(thank you, Bob Guccione)
we did it on the old
creaky bed upstairs
(we used to lie half asleep
up there summer mornings
and hear the birds
wake us up as the soft breeze
blew in the window and the curtains
brushed our
naked backs and faces)

we were hot and excited
I remember that we said
so what if we get pregnant
and on the way to the hospital
it was, I decided I could not live
with myself if we
did not name him
for my deceased brother
I even remember the turn we were on
scared shitless as I was

now here he lies
on the living room floor
afraid to go to bed at night
because of television
and here I am writing poems
about it
afraid of
everything else

let us say we can live here
together a while
let us be happy we were not afraid one time
not too long ago to find
a little time in this sad dying world for love

THE THREE-MINUTE EGG

for Mark

Your mom and I left the house
as soon as her water broke,
the little flood announcing your arrival
to the bedroom floorboard
that needed a good scrubbing anyway,

Debbie'd had a hard day at work teaching,
I had been at school
with my head in the usual
cloud,
we came home and had a roast
cooking in some of that awful rusty water
we had out on the farm
with a bunch of spuds
and carrots,

we were going to do exercises
when you decided to do some of your own
a month early
and join us where we stood
in our farmhouse bedroom
at the end of a day
at the beginning of our life
with you.

Today, about nineteen years later
you call me from your house
where you have moved in with your friends
and try to be nonchalant
as you always do

and then you get to the point
just as you always do
(you always interrupt to say
so what's your point?)

just as you did on your first night.
We drove the icy moon-covered road
to the room where good old
Dr. Nazi would deliver you
into the presence of the first
bad joke you would hear,

then we, your new Mom and Dad
came home days later
to roast rotted on the stove
and all the delicious potatoes
and carrots in that funky water.
Your point, which was to ask,
(you who hate to ask anything,
would not even let me show you
how to use a broom when you were two)

how to cook a soft-boiled egg
and so I tell you and you are surprised
it takes such a short time.
Perhaps you thought adulthood
was more difficult to control than this.

I tell you Yes, I think it's what they call
the three-minute egg,
we tell each other we love one another
and hang up the phones.

I finish lunch by myself in the kitchen
reading a book of poems,

in the ninth house we have lived in
since you were born

get into the 14th car
we have had to buy since then,

drive back
to the sixth full-time job
I have held since that night,

but what I didn't tell you is
it really takes longer than that.

ADD TO THAT LIST

that Mark my son and I now know
how to use a screwdriver to start a 1982 Chevy Citation
not that we would ever do that but that we did
today when we learned how to do it at the police impound lot,
for though he had the key, the key to his car
the car we've spent about roughly half a gazillion dollars on now
the key would not work, so the sixtyish woman
who took us out to where the car was parked on the lot
showed us how, but it needed a jump start, the battery
having been drained of all its power
although brand new a month ago,
because the kid who stole the car
to "joy-ride" as they call it, did not of course
worry, when he abandoned it, that if he did not press
the little sliding metal piece in the steering column assembly
all the way down, that the battery would drain, no,
he had not thought of that, nor of the 60 dollars we had to pay
to get the car out of impound though we had done no wrong
except to be stupid by leaving a car parked by our house
with a window broken out making it easy for him to get in
and steal the car and abandon it in Benson, so we
could come down to the impound lot and claim it, where Mark
could then get in and with the teaching of the impound lot lady
and a set of heavy-duty jumper cables, and with 60 dollars,
could drive the old car we bought for him back home
so that I was able to drive along behind him and see by the shape
of his head, or maybe by the way he held his head,
that he looked enough like his mother driving the Vega
across the western states from San Diego to Lincoln,
Nebraska, 23 years ago, 5 years before his birth,
that I would remark upon that to myself
while I drove behind him toward the house
on the street with the funny name "Pinkney," and look
at all the stickers he ruined his trunk lid with,

names of his favorite bands, Fugazi, Blenny, Revilo (his own)
and a couple others he put on like badges to say
not so much what kind of music he likes but who he is,
which did not stop the other young boy from taking his car,
whose few moment s of joy-riding in my son's car, I hope,
gave him joy, a joy he will never have that I had
riding along in the heavy pink & gray traffic toward home,
behind the impotent stickers, the rust,
the farting exhaust that needs a new muffler,
behind our only boy, who at one stop sign
pulls his arm that impossible way he does behind his head,
then lights and smokes a cigarette, and breathes that, in and out.

GREG KUZMA ☙

Born in 1944, Greg Kuzma is the author of *Song for Someone Going Away* (Ithaca House), *Good News* (Viking), *The Obedience School* (Three Rivers Press), and many other books. Recent long poems appeared in *Triquarterly*, *Harvard Review*, *Poetry East*, and *Witness*. He was educated at Syracuse University (BA, 1966, MA, 1967), he taught in the English Department at the University of Nebraska - Lincoln until his retirement and is the editor of *Best Cellar Press*.

Sandhills published the poems included here in *McKeever Bridge* (2002).

NOTE FROM KUZMA ABOUT SANDHILLS PRESS

Little did I know when I began *Pebble* and my The Best Cellar Press that they might lead to what Greg Kosmicki is doing at Backwaters Press and what Mark Sanders is doing with Sandhills Press. Back in the 60s there was a mass movement towards little magazines. I was not fully aware of how many enterprises were new or were starting up in those years. Although thinking back now I realize that I was buying the first issues of *Lillabulero* and *Apple* and others, right off the newstand at The Syracuse Book Center, I must have thought somehow that poetry and little magazines began with me, or somehow were hatched just in time so that I could participate in them. Like so many of my students today, for me time began when I first checked my watch.

It's difficult for me to appreciate how much easier everything is today. I am still locked into the past which had been such a fascinating present tense. With *Pebble* I purchased an old Chandler & Price platen press, 12x18, and stood next to it more or less as my father stood next to the gigantic metal lathe at his tool making shop at Oneida Limited. An oil can came with the press, as well as tons of type and iron chases and a paper cutter with a huge long lever like some instrument of torture. Print was made from metal, type cast in lead, or from linotype. Barb and I experimented with hand-set type... but the recreational printer I had purchased my press from had never redistributed the type he set for his many jobs, and though the jobs were tied in string, the long bumpy trip out to Crete, Nebraska broke them up. We must have had over 100 different fonts, but most of the drawers were nearly empty. For the first issue we printed, *Pebble 4*, Barb did set some poet names and poem titles, but the allure was not there. Later when Harry Duncan of Cummington Press fame printed two of my books, I got to see what true and good fine printing was. I never practiced this art... or rather all I did was practice it... getting better with every issue or pamphlet... until, by the mid seventies, I had reached almost the apprentice level.

I was in love with words, but also in love with the impressions type made when it pushed against soft paper. Some of the issues the imprints on the pages are so deep their registration will never relax. As well the paper cutter, when screwed tight, would leave its teeth marks on the covers as I flattened the issues. Printing and binding little books was physical work, the kind where there is sweat involved. And I flattened the springs of my car hauling trays of linotype out from Lincoln.

I remember how outraged I was when "offset printing" came along... and the ink lay on top of the sheet almost like a coffee stain or a flake of dust . . . .Printing for me meant stamping, or embossing... it was almost akin to working with chisels on marble, or even maybe granite. My father's love affair with steel and brass and copper came down to me, inherited, apparently, and my pride in my work must have been partly to show him I was not entirely inept, or merely just a book worm. The press itself was a monster, and still lodges in our basement (or cellar) in the same way Frost's Witch of Coos will never be free of "the bones up attic."

These things I talk of so accessibly here go back 40 years— one of the few pleasures I have in getting old. To live long enough that one's own past reads like an historical novel or a classic film. To think that books are built while staring at a screen... amazes me. And still, I hate to admit it, there is nothing to equal a letterpress book. At a reading in Brownville a few months back I happened to purchase a Scribner *Poets of Today* volume— which introduces not only Harry Duncan as a poet to the world, but May Swenson as well, my beloved May Swenson, and my dear friend and mentor Harry Duncan, who bears the name of my father. The book is solid and heavy and unevenly inked, and it has typos in it, and letters that came a bit loose and print slightly off center. In other words, it's a real book... and there is a textural experience reading it both with one's eyes and one's fingertips. Holding it in bed at night it's like my little bear I nearly wore the face off rubbing it-- it makes me feel safe.

The problem with the old laborious techniques is that few people were served by the process. We simply could not have the million books of poems a year we now have were people like me the ones who had to print and bind them. It would take Harry Duncan sometimes 8 or 9 months to set the type and print the signatures, then fold and trim and bind the copies of one book. And then make only 200 copies, the full press run. My *For My Brother* was printed with this size press run in 1981, and only Mark Sanders managed to review it. I don't know where the other copies went— perhaps to the collectors of Duncan's fine press work.

In saying this I come to the convergence of these two ideals. For me the beautiful printing of *For My Brother*, and its purple paper binding, and its double sheet pages, was an exquisite thing. And yet very much a private thing. I value the few copies I own in almost the same way I value the few things I own that Jeff made, a couple belt buckles of German silver, a beautifully ornate knife, with its sheath cut from some old LLBean leather boots.

But now on my desk beside me sit reprints of *For My Brother* from Lewis-Clark Press (a subsidiary of Sandhills Press). This book is as if "in print" for nearly the first time . . . or maybe my brother is dead again and mourned anew for others as well as for myself. One is the historical book, the other the rough house version that can fight for shelf space at the local used-book store. The first version makes me feel old, and sad too; the new version helps me feel young, and alive again to whatever redemption words can bring.

There are certainly numerous and almost infinite numbers of ways to connect to and love books. I'm reading now the tiny format Norton reprints of the Freud volumes originally printed by Virginia and Leonard Woolf's Hogarth Press. The Norton paperback format has tiny type. I have to squint to read it... as if in reading Freud I'm reading in the dark with a flashlight under the covers of my bed. Is Freud's voice more a squeak and less magisterial in this minimal format? Not at all. It's almost as if I'm holding in my hand the indestructible structure of DNA, so small and compact and yet so powerful it scares one to touch it. With any book the cover and the paper and the water stains well may be quaint and interesting in their object display, but it is the words which endure, words which hold the page or not, or jump into our memories or unconscious as the case may be.

For me there's not a single book that I do not hold dear. Maybe someday I'll be joined at the forehead to the computer monitor, and my hands worn down from typing, unable any longer to hold a book. For now printed books, in whatever format or design, remain a coherent and powerful link to hundreds of years of our lives lived in words and so preserved. I owe Mark Sanders and his great press the collection of my Adirondack Mountain poems in which my brother shares so much their darkness and their joy. There are so many of us served by presses of whatever size or scope. The books or pamphlets or "titles" we have done... sustain the ongoing dialogue between future and past. Best Cellar would be over 40 this year, were it alive and well. My brother would be 57. Sandhills Press is still ongoing, a young 30. We should all be glad.

ℰↄ

CROSSING RAQUETTE LAKE AT NIGHT

My father, wreathed in smoke,
changes places with me.
Neither sees. The shore

is all echo, of the motor
buzzing. And the two of us
dark in the folds of our clothes,
talk to the cold.

I think of the fish
below me
who must hear the motor
as something without predicament.
Or as the bird, nestled
inside its feathers,
hears us with regret.

Sometimes the shore is darker
than the lake, sometimes the
lake darker. Sometimes my father
as he shifts in the gloom
to get comfortable. The wind
tries to fill our eyes.

We would be traveling there still

on and on with the fish
listening and the bird falling
almost to sleep, had not
some woman turned up a lamp
in some place darker than ours.

THE CAMP IN EARLY SPRING

I found the beaver, broken
out of ice
with a frozen tail
stiff as a blackjack

but floating light as ice
a diagram in water
of the body's natural poise.

I found the house door shattered
by the weather that had howled there
all the months,
and deep inside
back in a corner
a branch had crawled
to hang on to its leaves.

The view had changed somewhat.
A tree I used to watch
had left its place along the point.
More smoke hung on the lip
of shore
where roads come in from other
places now.

Another winter
steadies in my bones.

FROM THE COVE

From the cove where my father has taken himself
To sit and think, I walk back out of luck.
The man won't talk. If he baits up at all
He casts hard trying to bruise the water.
From years ago I remember his fisherman's tricks,
The secret of the riffles, the lure of deep pools.
But there's nothing here now,
The fish have gone elsewhere,
And the water where he carried me in spring flood's
Down. He can't fix the bird nest in my reel,
His eyes have grown too thick to spot the
Loops in which I try to snare the hook.
He sits in his own cove while I patrol the stream
In search of fast water. His own father,
Of whom I have pictures,
Came here years ago and sat like he is now,
All day watching the sandwiches.

MY FATHER AND I STEAL
AN ENGINE FROM A SAWMILL

He hugged the engine to his leg
like a great boot.
It weighed him, weighed his mind.
With it he could not walk

but ran limping as if it were his boot
while I ran circles on the dirt
to hide unequal tracks.
The heaps of sawdust in the yard

reminded me of women's bodies,
the way the flesh caves in with age.
When wet, the sawdust heaps
resemble legs and breasts.

He hurried under them around them,
like a man outsexed,
grunting over now between his legs
the sheath which hid the engine

we would stick on some hard platform
much like what we took it from,
to rim a snowmobile he would not finish
anyway these past four years.

The engine sits bolted to a wasted thing
where once he carried it, a burden,
for two minutes in a lumber yard,
around which lay the waste of its own work.

HUNTING

There's a sweater of steam
around his face.
Every few seconds a whiter smoke
blooms through it.

My eyes are watering.
Their corners feel like glass.

I fill my pipe
from his tobacco pouch.
I heft it.
It feels good.

Nothing today
presents itself to be killed.

At the shore

we sit and watch the waves.

Shotgun on my shoulder,
pipe in my mouth,

follow the old man back
where we came from.

WITH MY BROTHER IN THE ADIRONDACKS

And we went there.

Q.   Why?

A.   Because we were young
      and the water boiled up
      over the rocks

      and there was a grassy spot
      to take a girl

      or eat a bologna sandwich
      hard boiled egg.

Q.   And you were happy?

A.   Yes. We were involved.

      The hands reached out
      the branch was there
      the sky was blue
      we lived in a cool breeze
      of the inevitable.

      "Gift" was the shouting
      of each bird.

Q.   What happened? Describe a trip.

A.   Typically there were two of us.
      My brother and 1.
      He did what I could not.
      I did the rest.
      He made the eggs.

I cut the wood.

He rowed the boat.
I caught the fish.
We both laughed.

Q.   And there was no trouble?

A.   Everywhere we went
       was our address.
       I slept not one bad night
       with even the rocks under me
       with even the snow, the rains.
       It seemed we were the children
       of the snow, the rain.

       If what you mean by trouble
       is were we hurt
       I tell you there was once

       I stopped to get my breath
       on a long climb up hill
       Jeff knew.

       I reached out for that breath
       and it was there.

Q.   So things were good?

A.   It seems then things were good.
       The grim catastrophe tomorrow would become
       had not yet turned its headlines
       in my heart.

       I said, if only to the wind,
       I am alive!
       And pitied everyone not in my shoes.
       My brother – who knows what he lived.
       But I was safe.

Q.   What was the river like, the River Kleeg?

A.   There was a turbulence in spots.
        There were big rocks,
        and pools behind that looked like maple syrup.
        One night a hatch of flies
        came off the flats.
        I lit a cigarette
        beside a tree,

        pissed on some lichens
        near the trail
        watching the steam rise.

        Among the overhang of branches
        near the stream
        we built the fire
        nestled in among the stones.
        It snapped in the night air
        from the sapped wood
        we fed it.
        Oh it talked, we let it.
        We let it do all the talking.

ALONG SOUTH INLET

(for my father)

In my mind you stand with creel
and rod, net and fishing vest,
decked out in pale green hip boots
the color of Scotch pine needles

in a clearing in the forest
where between us we have scattered
the worms in the first
minutes of dawn.

Upstream I see you thigh deep
already casting out

for some luck
a fish coming up beautiful

in your hand and eye
where I flounder to net him.
In the net he is bent like a
cucumber. I see further

the trail through bushes
mad as the stream where no man
could run in the dark and not die
holding you like a flower

when you stop to light your pipe,
while I, your boy who turns against you
in the end, waits for the smoke
to wreath your head and skull,

who now dreams of this ceremony
and says to himself
this is how I will want my children
to live their dreaming.

THE LOONS

I will lift up the tent to my back
and the boat too will I carry
having the shoes on my feet will aid me
having the wallet behind in the car
the bills coiled like snakes
in a cookie jar

will make me go swift on the rivers
uphill against rocks willI go
and the frying pan carried
to carry the meat of the trout

I will feel in the dark stream for
with the fishing line and the hook

which from my eye and my ear
I will keep with some magic maneuver
learned years ago from my father

and carry him too up the mountain
and my brother Jeff who is dead

I will eat in the morning his breath
and his extra pancake
there on the shore of the lake

he showed me the year of his death
when he took me
and we sat on the lake in the sun
alive in that grand morning

and the axe I will carry against
the trees so that the fire be fed
up into gorgeous flames

making the place I have come
lighting the dark of the mind
into the present occasion.
All night the loons will be calling
speaking the voice beyond sweat
beyond muscle
speaking of aching for all that is missing.

DAVID LEE ∞

David Lee was named Utah's first Poet Laureate and has been honored with grants from the National Endowment for the Arts and the National Endowment for the Humanities; he has received the Mountains & Plains Booksellers Award in Poetry and the Western States Book Award in Poetry. Books include: *A Legacy of Shadows: Selected Poems* (Copper Canyon Press, 1999); *News from Down to the Cafe: New Poems* (Copper Canyon Press, 1999); *Twentyone Gun Salute* (Grey Spider Press, 1999); *The Fish* (Wood Works Press, 1997); *Wayburne Pig* (Brooding Heron Press, 1997); *Covenants* (with William Kloefkorn) (Spoon River Poetry Press, 1996); *Paragonah Canyon* (Brooding Heron Press, 1990); *Day's Work* (Copper Canyon Press, 1990); *The Porcine Canticles* (Copper Canyon Press, 1984); *Shadow Weaver* (Brooding Heron Press, 1984); *Driving and Drinking* (Copper Canyon Press, 1979); and *The Porcine Legacy* (Copper Canyon Press, 1974). He recently retired as the Chairman of the Department of Language and Literature at Southern Utah University.

"Mean" appeared in *The Decade Dance* (1991).

NOTE FROM LEE ABOUT SANDHILLS PRESS

30 years. That's technically a generation, which places Sandhills Press in the very elite, longevitywise, of non-vanity American poetry small presses. I have a god's ransom of respect for Mark Sanders and Sandhills Press. I admire the editorial acumen, artistic design and layout of the books, and more importantly the integrity, perseverance and willingness to take a chance on emerging and unknown poets that Sanders has continually displayed. America and American poetry could well use more Sandhills Presses.

∞

MEAN

HELL HATH NO FURY
LIKE A SOW WITH PIGS

1

Pretty soon now I sed and
John nods his head, watching
so I sed I see she's broke the sack
there's water and his head goes up and down
again but he doesn't say anything
so we both stand and watch
John's big white sow back in her shed
while she breathes easy
seven hundred pounds sprawled across yellow straw
finally John sez any time now
and I nod my head this time
he sez yep just any time
but the only thing we can do is watch
so we stand and wait
and watch John's white sow labor
and John lights a cigarette
to help the time go by while we watch

2

Last time sez John she went craziern hell
I had her in that pen with a wood floor
I put in a lamp for the cold and
she's half done and got up that mean sonofabitch
she done went over and bit that lectric wire
and it shocked her or something
she went like a crazy woman to banging
her head on the walls and floor
and hollered like a elephant shot in the butt
with buckshot she tore hell out of that pen
and had two more pigs while she's standing up and
never knew it she acted like she's blind
and couldn't see nothing I had to get

them pigs out with a rake or she'd of stomped
on them all she jerked that rake
right out of my hand twicet I had
to get it back with a stick sos I could get
them pigs out or they'd be dead
I got all but one that she killed
and she finally went over and lain down
to have her pigs again but ever time
one of them I had out squolt she'd jump up
and go crazy again I had to put them pigs
in the front of my pickup all night
to make her be still and that light
never did work after that she ruint it
so I sez how come you keep her John?
she's too big and mean and John
looks at me like I was nuts or something
he sed cause she had twelve pigs and raised
all but one more besides the one she stomped
that's why, wouldn't you? but I didn't
say anything, John's white sow was too mean
for me, I would have sold her to John
if she was mine but she wasn't
she was already John's so I didn't have to

3

John I sez after a while because she wouldn't pig
I'll bet that sow's got a pig stuck breech
and it won't come but John looks over
at his pickup and doesn't say anything
so I say if she does and it doesn't come
it could kill her and all them pigs too
don't you think? but he keeps looking at
his pickup so I say I don't know of course
but that might be it she's been in labor
a long time and she broke her water
before I got here I saw the last of the wet
when I came but I don't know she's not my sow
it might not be that but John sez real low
she throwed Carl out of the pen that time

he got in and tried to climb out after him
she'd of killed him if she'd got to him
so I decided I wouldn't say anything else
she was John's sow and he'd know what to do

4

Why don't you get in there and look
sez John you know more about that than I do
and I sez no I don't John and I have
to be getting home pretty soon Jan will be
getting worried and I hate to keep
her up John sez Dave I'll give you twenty-five
dollars if you'll go get that pig out and
I sez John I'm not getting in that pen with
that sow for a hundred dollars John sez
okay fifteen dollars cash I sez no John
I'm not going to get in there for a thousand
dollars John sez I'll give you a pig
I sez I wouldn't do it for the sow and all
the pigs loaded up to take to the auction
John sez okay a live pig and you can pick it
but I sed no and I meant it
not for all his pigs and I acted like I
was getting ready to leave
It wasn't I wanted to see how it came out
but I wasn't getting in that pen
so John goddamned me and sed I was a sissy
and I didn't say anything because John was right

5

John sez if I get in there will you come
and hold the lantern in the door so I can see?
and I sed yas because the sow was in
bad shape by then we could see that and
she had to have help but I sed John
if she comes after me I'm getting out
and I'm not going to worry about the lantern
getting out with me so it may get busted

John sez if she gets up you just make sure
you don't get in my way or she'll get you
and the lantern both and I sed okay
because I knew there's no way John
can get out of that pen before me
I wasn't worried about that
so I sed where's the lantern? John sez
over here so we go to his pickup
for the lantern and John gives me the lantern
and some clean rags to hold then
he gets in his jockey box and pulls out
a pistol I sez what's that? and John sez
it's a gun and I sez oh I see and he sez
I aint getting in there with her without no
gun my mama didn't raise no idiots
and if I need this I want to have it
with me that's why and he put it in
his coat pocket and I didn't say anything
because it wasn't my sow she was John's

6

John climbed in the pen and I followed
he went in the shed with the sow but I
stayed in the door while he moved around
behind her slow to see what she'd do
she had her eyes closed and breathed
hard because she hurt so bad
and I shined the light in so John could see
John knelt down behind her and touched her
but she didn't move so he rolled up his sleeve
and started in to see what was wrong
breech? I whispered and he nodded so
I was right and John went in to try and get it out
John whispers hold still I caint see
and I sez who? and he sez you and
I saw the lantern was shaking I was scared
so I held it with both hands and it
was still John twisted his hand inside the sow
and he sed I got it I'm gone take it out now

he started pulling his arm back and the
pig came out and it was breech
got it? I sed and John sez yas gimme a rag
and I leaned in to hand him a towel and
the pig wiggled in his hand John tried to grab
its mouth but the pig squealed in his hand

7

Goddam you John screamed
the white sow jumped up and bellowed
so loud the tin roof on the shed shook
and jerked around toward John
I stood there like Lot's wife shining the light in
John screams goddam you again
and jumps back against the back wall
of the shed and hits it so hard it should have
come down holding the pig tight against his chest
the sow roars at him the muscles
in her body standing out all the hair on
her back straight up and I think drop that pig
John but I can't say anything I'm frozen
holding the lantern in the door
the sow roaring and John screaming
then he tears at his pocket and pulls out
the pistol goddam you he yells you get away from me
you sonofabitch and the sow barks loud like a maddog
the size of a jersey cow
John points the pistol at her head and it shakes
like an aspen limb in springtime
goddam you and she screams again
snick snick snick snick snick snick snick
I see the empty cylinder turn as John pulls
the trigger and I taste powder in my mouth
drop it! I hear somebody say
John keeps pulling the trigger yelling goddam you
the sow roars and her shoulders bunch up in a knot
she's so mad she's slobbering
DROP IT I yell again and John looks at me
his eyes wide as hubcaps

DROP THAT PIG I scream and I see John's
hand loosen and the pig falls to the ground
but he keeps pulling the trigger snicksnicksnick
the pig hits on its back and lays there
and the sow lowers her head and looks at it
but keeps on grunting loud and mean and fast
John stops pulling the trigger but keeps the pistol
pointed at her head and the pig gets up
and starts moving the sow quits grunting and
sniffs it then looks at John and barks again
John pulls the trigger again but he can't
say anything anymore and the sow turns and lays down
and grunts and another pig pops out
the first pig finds her and tries to find a teat
and the second pig squirms and shakes its head and
tries to clear its nose and John stands with
the pistol pointed at the sow and I stand
holding the lantern and the sow grunts to her pigs
just like we're not there and nothing happened
and I say John? and John points the pistol at me
I say get out John and he sez what?
and I say get out of that shed John before
she gets up and John sez who? and I say
get out of there John and John looks at the sow
and points the pistol at her and he starts
sliding around the wall and we get out
of John's mean white sow's pen

8

John's shaking so hard he can't light
a cigarette so I do it but he drops it on
the floorboard and I pick it up and put it
in his mouth and he smokes
I say you got a beer? and he sez in the back
I think so I take the lantern and look
and he has some hid in his junk in the bed
I get it and for a long time we drink beer
and don't say anything and I see that my hands
are shaking so the beer foams out the top of my can

so I drink three fast so it won't
and I don't know if he ever finished his
finally I sed John I wouldn't have a pig like that
I'd get rid of her if she's mine she's just too mean
she's gonna kill somebody someday
John's staring straight ahead through the window
the muscles in his face still tight, drawn
he sez goddammit that's too bad
and I sed well you can't help it some go mean
he sez she was a good sow I sez she's okay now
John sez but it was her or me and I sez it's okay
he sips his beer then sets it on the dashboard
and leans back and I see tears in his eyes and
he's still staring straight ahead through the windshield
she was a good sow he sez even if she was mean
goddammit I hated having to shoot her like that
and I looked out the window and didn't
say anything. She was John's sow, not mine.

Kelly Madigan ₔ

Kelly Madigan is the award-winning author of *Getting Sober: A Practical Guide to Making it Through the First 30 Days* (McGraw-Hill, 2007). She is also an accomplished poet and essayist whose work has been published in literary magazines and anthologies such as *Best New Poets 2007, Crazyhorse, Prairie Schooner, Barrow Street, The Massachusetts Review, Calyx, Natural Bridge*, and elsewhere. Kelly is a 2008 recipient of the National Endowment for the Arts Fellowship in Creative Writing.

Sandhills published her *Born in the House of Love* in its Main-Traveled Roads Chapbook series in 2005; these two poems come from that collection.

ₔ

BORN IN THE HOUSE OF LOVE

Tree limbs groaned aside
to make way. The salt river poured
over my head. My iris constricted
without knowing that it could.

Still I wasted my body
on the world. Handed my keys to men
with mud clamped to their boots.
Drew putty into my air sacs,
holding my breath until it dried.
Turned the soft crook of my arm up
to the needle's bite. Rode on the shoulders
of drunken boys who could not
keep their balance in the dark.

We are each holier than we know,
tumbling ourselves against tectonic edges

like glass beads, clearing and clarifying
until the world, when the light has a certain slant,
can see its unguarded face right through us.

WHAT THE WORLD CALLS HABIT

It was never the cigarette itself that mattered so much
as the practiced movements my muscles memorized,
the way my fingers knew how to hold the delicate paper-
wrapped cylinder, or how to snap flint to start the lighter.
It was in these tiny gestures that the addiction hid itself,
intertwined with tendon, resting on breath, worming in
until what the world calls habit felt instead like a way
of being in the world, familiar as gait. And sometimes
it wasn't even that so much as the clean space the cigarette
left in the pack, a perfect shape next to the round shoulders
of its siblings, always the same size and unlike the long
unbearable days, small enough to know how to fill.

KATHLEEN NORRIS ɛↄ

Kathleen Norris is a best-selling poet and essayist. She became known for her writings about Christian spirituality, especially after she became a Benedictine oblate and spent two extended periods at Saint John's Abbey in Minnesota. Born in Washington D.C., Norris was raised in South Dakota and Honolulu, attended Bennington College in Vermont, and now divides her time between South Dakota and Hawaii. She was married to the poet David Dwyer until his death in 2003.

These poems were included in *The Decade Dance* (1991).

ɛↄ

EVE OF ST. AGNES IN THE HIGH SCHOOL GYM

The saint's been dead too long;
no young girl keeps her vigil. Not one fasts
or prays tonight, for a vision
of the one she'll marry.

A band plays—too loudly—
popular tunes a few years out-of-date.
Young men emerge from a huddle
of team-mates, cheerleaders,
fans. They run onto the court,
howling, slapping hands.

Men just a few years older
stand smoking by the door;
their windbreakers advertise a local bar.
Others sit in the stands,
holding sleepy children;
the women with them look worried and tired

Snow falls silently,
snaking through the streets.
The game takes place in both past and future.

Done up like spring
in a pale yellow skirt
and lavender sweater,
a pretty girl sleepwalks
on high heels. She carries herself
to a boy on the bench
who doesn't look up; and the old men sigh.

When the game is over
they flee on the storm.
The saint sits in heaven,
and if anyone's praying
on this chilly night,
let it be for love.

Land of the Living

(for Basil Atwell, O.S.B.)

Menstruation is primitive:
no getting around that fact, as
I wipe my blood from the floor
at 3 A.M. in the monastery guest room,
alone in this community
of sleeping men.

Once again, I have given up
the having of children.
I celebrate instead
a monthly flowering
of the not-to-be,
and let it go without regret.

Earlier tonight, a young monk
splashed my face with holy water;
we both laughed. Then, just as unexpectedly,

he flew down a banister, and
for one millisecond
was an angel—robed,
without feet—
all irrepressible joy
and good news.

The black madonna watched us,
expectant as earth just plowed.

My sister holds her baby
in a photograph. They smile at me
from the mirror I've placed them on.
Lili sits like the Christ Child
on her mother's lap. She sits very straight
in a blood-red dress
and stares into something
that makes her look amused, and wise.

It's here, in the land of the living,
the Psalm says we shall see God's goodness.
Yes: my whole body is weeping
but I'm glad to be here,
a useless woman
sleepless and kept waiting
as breath keeps coming,
as the blood flows.

YOUNG LOVERS WITH PIZZA

The curve of a smile,
a hip;
clothes everywhere,
pizza in a box, laughter
when the telephone intrudes
and you must untangle
legs, breasts, hips
to answer it.
It becomes

a private joke:
the person on the other end
doesn't know a thing.

I envy you,
couples in this town,
in the world:
that first touch, growing,
the dry, breathy heat
and kisses like cool water,
couples lost for a moment
inside each other, inside out.

Don't think of me,
or of your duty
to God and telephone.
The air makes even
a man's hard body
soft to touch,
the breasts
of even a small woman
generous. Listen,
the earth curves,
the light curves gently
around your smiles and
your naked hips, holding
everything you need.

HILDA RAZ ℰↃ

Hilda Raz was born in Rochester, New York, educated at Boston University, and moved to Nebraska in 1963. She was a professor of English and women's and gender studies at the University of Nebraska - Lincoln, where she was Glenna Luschei Endowed Editor of *Prairie Schooner*, until her retirement. Her books include *Trans* (Wesleyan UP, 2001), *What is Good* (Thorntree Books), *The Bone Dish* (State Street Press), *Divine Honors* (Wesleyan UP, 1998), and written in collaboration with her son, Aaron Raz Link, *What Becomes You*, a work of creative nonfiction on gender. She is the editor of several anthologies, including *Living in the Margins: Women Writers on Breast Cancer* (Persea Books, 2000), *The Best from Prairie Schooner: Fiction and Poetry* (U of Nebraska P, 2001), *The Best from Prairie Schooner: Personal Essays* (U of Nebraska P, 2000), co-edited with Kate Flaherty, *The Prairie Schooner Anthology of Contemporary Jewish American Writing* (1998). Her two children are John Link, a composer and professor at William Paterson College in New Jersey, and Aaron Link, a jeweler, mask maker, and biologist who works in Portland, Oregon.

"Drought: Benedict, Nebraska" and "Fast Car on I-80" appeared in *The PlainSense of Things 2: Eight Poets from Lincoln, Nebraska* (1997); "My Dream, Your Dream" and "Three Ways of Looking at It" were published in *The Decade Dance* (1991).

ℰↃ

MY DREAM, YOUR DREAM

In half-light salt
crusted in my eye
corners but I haven't
been weeping, only
traveling in a country
where you come careening
around a corner on your bicycle, wind a wall
you've smashed into,
far side of your face
gone flat on the bone.
I reach to wake you up
to me but you say *no*
and turn into a half-light
of your own, hair a crest
on the pillow and you're
heading into blue rain
rising fast over the windy
crescent of some western hill.

THREE WAYS OF LOOKING AT IT

Having been given permission to write
hooks into the soft portions of cheeks
I write this down on a morning of trees
cracked, chimneys felled, decimation
the old way, by lot, limbs torn from trunks,
sockets exposed; stumps partially
uprooted, fracture everywhere
no glistening, no green haze:
hopeless December, month of death
like all the others.

Tension demands a second stanza
whose blossoms toss on branches
upward into the summer air
in the fists of lovers

whose gesture signifies triumph,
union. Even the sun is singed, fused
with the blazing sky.

And I am sitting in a neutral season,
autumn in the window, washed now and
again by shudders of wind,
now the throat catch, the faltering
lungs, now the heart beating
triumphantly if irregularly loud:
see me, see me sitting here,
still alive, see this ordinary
impermanent, failed winner?

DROUGHT: BENEDICT, NEBRASKA

Merce says, it don't do to get too attached to any of 'em,
her grandson for example, he's four—you might lose them.

In 1972 she come home from town, some fool party
or other, to find her husband lying on the floor
under the kitchen table. You can't hide from me,
she said, I can see your feet. But he didn't move.

Nothing worse than that, except the tornado
that come right after, her sisters driving out of town
after dropping her off on the porch, not moving—
must have been a swirl in the middle of that wind,
the vacuum, that kept them still though the tires rolled,
she could see it, until the car got loose inches only farther south,
and got away. Meanwhile she called mama two houses down.

When the neighbor seen her running in the road, she come too.
Then the kids from the farm, and Judy from York, her girl
just back from the hospital with tonsils, wrapped up in a quilt
(like the doctor said). We all went into the storm cellar
and Juddy, my oldest, insisted on pushing up the door
just as the funnel passed, so his boys could see it go
—David still on the kitchen floor, they wouldn't let me touch him

before the doctor—and all of us there for half an hour
till it passed, the sheriff's men stationed one at each corner
of the section to watch for the ambulance.

Later on the porch the family around, all afternoon I leaned
over the railing and heaved and gagged—just nerves, was all it was.
I hope I don't have to go through that again,
but that's what a life's for, I guess, they say the Lord
don't put more on a soul than she can bear.

Merce fills my cup with good Swede coffee, starts the breakfast dishes.
She's eighty and I'm just up from an operation, teaching my first class
in spring. The grey sky promises rain and believe me, we need it.

FAST CAR ON NEBRASKA I-80: VISITING TEACHER

Early sun on fields.
A pheasant flushes and skims
the north ditch on air.
Students, I say out loud, rehearsing
in the car, *this morning
our subject is nouns,
how to pin them down.
Gold is the color of freedom,*
I say, *the fields Mennonites farm
to yield more than an acre can.*

Later, the most compelling noun
is *car,* fast skimming away from a class
I've asked to describe death
in terms of silk tatters, the smoking gun, for example,
of a brother shooting over his sister's head.

The girl in the front row
who daubed her eyelids purple
wrote about *the-one-who-is-gone,*
meaning her sister. And wrote
about *the-one-who-did-it,*

meaning her brother who shot the gun,
whom she ought to hate–and doesn't.

She doesn't. She misses the black hair
of his head, his brown eyes, her sister's
pale skin, now gone *dead-white.*
I don't make her read out loud.

First things they said, this is a Mennonite community
and a boy killed his sister here two weeks ago.
But they forgot to mention the family, other kids in school.

Early Monday, driving through wet air at seven
I'd noticed the horizon did a good job
on my heavy mind: what had seemed a knot
so snarled I couldn't get a nail in
began to unwind as I watched through the windscreen.

Here, the town is groomed, each stubble lawn smooth
in a yellow fallow. The houses are brick.
Each child in grades two through twelve
is clean and well-dressed. Some seniors
they tell me in class, drive Thunderbirds,
or go visit China in the summer. In the library
I have a glassed-in office usually reserved
for the Monday-Wednesday speech teacher.
I work undisturbed. Nowhere here
is violence I can see, only the peace of community.

Not here, or in the deep ditches where pheasant harbor,
or the deer. Who couldn't be happy here?

Marjorie Saiser 🙰

Marjorie Saiser´s is a poet living in Lincoln, Nebraska. She received an MA in creative writing at the University of Nebraska - Lincoln, winning the Vreelands Award and the Academy of American Poets competition. Her work has been published in literary journals including *Prairie Schooner*, *Georgia Review*, *Zone 3*, *CrazyHorse*, and *Cream City Review*. Her poems have been finalists for the Robert Penn Warren Prize, the New Letters Literary Awards, and nominated for the Pushcart Prize. She is a 2000 recipient of the Merit Award from the Nebraska Arts Council and in 1999 received the Literary Heritage Award from the Nebraska Literary Heritage Association. Her first full length collection, *Bones of a Very Fine Hand*, won the Nebraska Book Award for poetry in 2000. Her second book, *Lost in Seward County*, was published in 2001 by Backwaters Press. She is co-editor of *Times of Sorrow, Times of Grace* (Backwaters Press, 2002), an anthology of poetry and prose by women of the Great Plains, which was named Poetry Honor Book in 2003 by the Nebraska Center for the Book, and also co-editor of a book of interviews, *Road Trip: Conversations with Writers* (Backwaters Press, 2003).

Note from Saiser About Sandhills Press

Every once in a while I go through my bookshelves because they are overflowing. I see what's there, what I'm saving, what I haven't culled out yet, what's lasting. I don't make it through all the shelves. It never fails; I begin to read. The volume that stopped me this last foray was *We have always been coming to this morning*, by Greg Kosmicki. Thank you, Sandhills Press, for this slim important book. These poems do me good, show me what I'm living for, show me that my tablecloth is my flag, the flag of the friendly country, and that I want you to come and join me and have bread and lasagna with my family. And only a few hours ago I was ranting at my over-religious relatives who want to bomb.

I see Sandhills Press has also hung in there with Barbara Schmitz's *How to Get Out of the Body*. And here's *On Common Ground* and *The Margin-*

alist and *The Plain Sense of Things*.   Oh, I'll be ranting and depressed again soon, but for now I'm encouraged to do what I'm supposed to do: put pen to paper, make it matter.

ॐ

A Man in Love with Wind

(for Don Welch)

A man in love with wind
held a noun in his hand
to admire the layers of its feathers,

the gold ring of its eye.
He spoke to it, hoping it heard. He tossed it
up onto a shelf of air,

where it opened and
rolled into flight: upstroke, downstroke.
It left him. Wherever he went, he listened
for the one that would circle, the one

that even in the dark would land,
would delicately place its weightless
claws on the shingles,
as if someone in the house lay awake to hear
the small impossible sounds that mean
home,

home.

Washing the Walls

My daughter wants things clean, wants me to
leave my shoes at the door. She's nesting, a bird
or a mammal pulling out feathers or fur to make
the nest round, warm. She is large and tired,
the child always before her. This is a way

I love her: I'm on a ladder
washing the walls,
on a ladder washing windows,
my hand over the ledges and sills
and floors of her house,
my hand across the glass
back and forth, corner to corner to corner.

Tonight she reads me comics and editorials
while I dust the blinds. I laugh until it hurts
behind my ears. Another joke, another slat.
We talk about the time I was pregnant with her.
She wants to know these things,
how she fits in, how her child fits in;
she is fierce to prepare the bed
and the clothes for him,
the books and music. She sits
cross-legged before her shelves
and shows me what she has,
what is ready. Once she pulled

her luggage down the streets of
Oxford before sunrise to the Greenline
bus stop. After cold cereal at the landlady's,
the sound of the wheels of her suitcase
on the sidewalk to the bus and then the plane.
All that day in my mind
I watched the winter storms, her path unlit
until it opened like a fallopian tube to a place
where I waited to gather her, safe and home,

waited as now she waits. She touches her belly,
her fingers circling, keeping the searchlight on,
sweeping the dark. It's her child. Nobody

will love him as she does, watching his progress
over the pole, the strong winds at the higher
elevations, the crackpots in the airports
with guns and explosives and axes to grind,
nobody assigned to the child as she is assigned.

My gift: these moist surfaces,
the shine of the wood,
the peppermint soap in the rag,
my hand moving
along the baseboards,
drawing boundaries,
my hand washing the walls,
this for the love of her

who lay in the dark of my body
as now, still, the thought of her
lies light and steady where
hope is, where it stays, where it lives.

HOW TO SURVIVE THE WINTER

tell Babe next door
in his air force parka leaning over
his garbage cans
that it is a mean one today

he will say you ain't seen
anything yet promise him a game of
sheephead promise him dominoes

remove your glove
scratch the lines and patches as they
take form on the inside of the windshield

turn the knob to something like cremate

at the red light a jogger
in a surgical mask will graze
the hood of your car

bless him

tell the woman in geier's
the wind is bad today

she will tell you she has been
watching the flag on the bank
since it was light enough to see
fluttering straight south like a goddam compass

hesitate between the hungarian tea ring and a
mixture of bismarks and crispies

take two dozen

the librarian will tell you of her
sister-in-law writing from California it
hasn't been so good there either

pay the fine

the bismarks and crispies will
sweeten the air of the car
sweet oil
sweet white creme
frosting thin as eucharist

between the pale yellow spaces of the
dough a warm
a soft
the only home
a welcome
a waiting

the kitchen air will flow about
your cheeks burning them

throw the coat on the table

wear red pajamas

settle into the pillows
denting them like the first bite
into a creme-filled roll

remember the yellow quilt in the
storeroom but do not get up
open the book to no particular chapter
begin anywhere

MARK SANDERS &

Poet, essayist, story writer, and editor Mark Sanders is a Nebraska native, born in Creighton in 1955 and raised on the eastern rim of the Sandhills in Ord. He holds a BA and MA in English from Kearney State College, a PhD in Modern Poetry from the University of Nebraska - Lincoln, and a PhD in Higher Education Leadership from the University of Idaho. He has taught in Nebraska high schools and at Southwest Missouri State University, Tarkio College, the University of Nebraska - Lincoln, Nebraska Wesleyan University, Southwestern Oklahoma State University, College of the Mainland, the University of Houston - Clear Lake, and at Lewis-Clark State College in Lewiston, Idaho; he is currently Chair and Professor of English at Stephen F. Austin State University in Nacogdoches, Texas. His poems, stories, and essays have been published in journals in the U.S., Canada, Great Britain, and Australia. His creative prose has appeared in such journals as *Glimmer Train, Shenandoah, South Dakota Review, North Dakota Quarterly*, and *River Teeth*, and among the journals that have published his poems are *Prairie Schooner, Poetry East, Tar River Poetry, Midwest Quarterly, Dalhousie Review, Poetry Wales*, and numerous others. His books include *Before We Lost Our Ways, The Suicide, Here in the Big Empty, Riddled with Light: Metaphor in the Poetry of W.B. Yeats, Conditions of Grace: New and Selected Poems*, and *Landscapes, with Horses*. He has been the editor of Sandhills Press since 1979, which includes the imprints Main-Traveled Roads Press, Talking River Publications (through 2008), and (with his wife Kimberly Verhines as Series Editor) Lewis-Clark Press. One of Sanders' stories, published in *Glimmer Train*, was given honorable mention as one of "100 other outstanding stories in 2006" in the 2007 edition of *Best American Short Stories*, edited by Stephen King; he is also the 2007 recipient of the Mildred Bennett Award from the Nebraska Center for the Book.

An earlier version of "Why Guineas Fly" was published in *A Dissimulation of Birds* (2002). "Bladen, Nebraska" was featured, in an extremely early version, in *The Sandhills and Other Geographies* (1980); this version appeared in *The PlainSense, I*, as did "Oasis Bar," "Plain Sense," and "The Creighton Pool Hall." "Sitting on Foth's Roof, with Beer" appeared in *The Decade Dance.*

WHY GUINEAS FLY

Malcom swung on the front gate, holding onto the frame's top and watching his feet glide an inch above the sidewalk that led up to his grandmother's house. He had finished his lunch—a casserole of home-made noodles with Star-Kist Tuna, a wash of green KoolAid. As always, his old maid aunts, bent on washing dishes and returning to *Guiding Light* and *Somerset*, had chased him out of the house with the slop bucket of table scraps to feed the pigs. He had lugged it to the pen and dumped its contents into the squeal-and-grunt riot. Now, the bucket sat outside the yard gate, and a congress of flies buzzed in and around it. By the next morning, maggots and their rancid slime would coat the pail, and he would smell again the sweet nausea. That same smell was all over the farm, in the barn layered deep in manure, in the hog wallow, in the dump in the trees, in the granary where green-white mold lay in the corners, among the sacks of fertilizer. While it was not one of the reasons he liked staying at his grandmother's, it was, at least, an indispensable detail of summer vacation.

Back and forth, he rode the gate's swing over the sidewalk, too old at fourteen to engage in such child's play, but summer must have its casual fill where it might, as it might. He closed his eyes, and behind the veil of his lids, he saw the bright red the August sunlight made, intense, like his uncle's rage; deep, like a well, where a dropped stone fell so long the splash was never heard; a brave heart, the world at war, the flames danc-ing up amid the explosions of bombs. There he was, flying through the midst of it, unscathed, fearful, but flying against fear.

The previous summer, a cottonmouth had found him here, riding the gate then, as now, his eyes shut, the red there, and—during the flight's descent—he heard a hissing like steam escaping from a radiator, some-thing sonorous that shook his senses, something sight-needful. Malcom opened his eyes. There the snake was, all five feet of it, coiled, its head drawn back. He leapt away from the gate, as if it were a pool spring-board, landing in a backward run toward the house to tell. The snake had struck just as Malcom leapt. And missed.

Grandma Geslar and his aunts, Vera and Dena, stood with Malcom at a safe distance as the snake uncoiled and sunned itself at the sidewalk's end. In the distance, they listened for the Model H Farmall, signaling his uncle Bob's return from the field to the house. At last, the tractor's *put-sput-put-sput* grew louder from behind the hill—then, Bob's capped head came into sight first, then the tractor, then the planter behind it. Dena left by the side gate to meet her brother, rushing between the dilapidated tool shed which leaned against a hackberry trunk and the garage where an old Ford Coupe that had not run in twenty years sat. She caught him just as he climbed down the tractor and his feet hit the dust of the farm-yard. Malcom could not hear what Dena was saying, but her arms flew, like pheasants flushed from refuge. Bob walked to the strawberry patch where a flat hoe leaned against the fence's wire mesh. He came back to make war against the snake.

The snake struck at the hoe each time Bob tried to pin the head. Sometimes, the snake made its motion toward Bob, who did a fat-dance backward, cursing, "Goddammit, you sonbitch!" The snake's mouth was white-gray; it reared its head high, balancing, menacingly.

"You be careful, there, Bob," his mother said.

Bob thrust the hoe at the snake again and again, at last rolling it just enough, and the man was on top of it, the hoe planted against the neck. The snake's body whipped and flailed, the tail-end looping around Bob's leg. Bob pressed hard upon the hoe handle, all his 250 pounds pushing.

"Don't let it get away!" Vera warned. "It'll get you."

"No, it won't," Bob wheezed, sweat all over his face. Then, the snake's head came loose. Bob putted it away with the hoe-head, as if he were playing croquet. The snake's length writhed and twisted, rolled in the dirt, and guineas, fearing the body but smelling blood, rushed over to pick at the red dust. When the body moved, the birds jumped back, wings lifting them. Then, they gathered their courage, approached again and again, dipping their hooked beaks into the soil-clotted globules. Running with the blood, heads low, their voices whirred like bedsprings.

Malcom loved the guineas, their oddity, their ugliness, from their gray-speckled football bodies, to the leathery masks they wore on their faces. And their noise—Jesus, what noise! Whenever something scared them, they would fly to the treetops or run, heads down like bombers coming in, and cry like alarms. They would have dropped no bombs; their rule for engagement was to avoid engagement. Had Malcom been a guinea, he would have flown when the snake appeared—he tried, but, earthbound boy that he was, he leapt and ran for all he was worth, one word floating in one syllable from his frightened mouth: "Snake!" His heart pumped hard, and that was thrilling. But he felt conspicuous in his inability to say more than he had.

He said nothing more during the entire snake-fighting episode. He had stood there, among his female relatives, watching, saying silence. His heroic uncle fought the demon, tempted the fangs, and, victorious, brought off its head, a country Galahad. Bob picked up the snake's body and draped it over the garden fence—a trophy that still moved for a half hour in the habit of muscle. Then, more carefully, he probed the head with a stick and showed the family the fangs. "Lookit here," Bob said. "Pretty damned nasty, ain't they?"

Malcom had seen nothing like it. The fangs, he knew from all the books he had read, meant he had been inches away from death. Death had laid its coils right at his feet, like a trip-rope that had not sprung only because he stepped a different direction. Death had set its intent upon his legs or feet; he would have walked out of this world, falling into what might be a poisoned next. Death was always too close. This time a snake, next time a fall from the hayloft, getting caught in a baler, slipping beneath the hooves of cows. Life was merely the action of side-stepping, the guinea alarm, and breath nothing more than a systematic thrust of a hoe handle.

Over supper, the kitchen hazy in the glow of an Aladdin's lamp—Malcom's grandmother hated to spend money on the REA—Bob kept talking about the snake. "Did you see how that sucker kept fighting me? I used to see snakes overseas during the war—they had coral snakes in the islands, and those bastards—'scuse the French—would come up and chew on people when they slept. Hung up hammocks to keep 'em away. Them that couldn't find a hammock set their cot legs inside big ol' coffee cans and such filled with gasoline. The snakes didn't like the smell of gas, I guess, though how those suckers smell, anyway? They got no noses."

Malcom found his entry into the conversation. "They smell through their tongues," he said. "I read about it."

"How they do that?" Bob questioned, displeased that his story was interrupted.

Malcom shrugged his shoulders, indicating his not being certain. "There's some sort of organ on the tips of the tongue's forks. Somehow it works."

"Well, anyway, the snakes wouldn't come near the cans, and no one in our group got bit. But, in the morning, we'd find big ol' spiders and centipedes floating in the gas. We'd dig 'em out and light them dead suckers. They popped and hissed, just like bacon getting crispy." Malcom smiled at his uncle, smiled at the image of incinerated bugs.

His uncle continued: "The only problem with the gas is that it stunk, and we had to be real careful about smoking. I tell you, we could have made toast of ourselves."

Dena and Vera kept their eyes lowered to their food, eating in polite silence, offering nothing to the conversation. Their forks and spoons moved fried potatoes, meat loaf, and home-grown green beans to their mouths.

"Were there any fires?" Malcom asked his uncle.

"I said we were careful. You listening?"

Malcom nodded. "How many of the soldiers got bit by snakes?"

"I dunno. But I bet it was bunches."

"How many in your camp?" Malcom asked—again.

"Did I say I didn't know?" Bob glared at Malcom. The guinea in his heart flew to a tree; an alarm crackled in his head. If Malcom were not careful, the next thing Bob would say would be harsh, a verbal slap, or, for that matter, a real one. Bob had done something extraordinary that day, and Malcom's persistent inquiry was ruining his pleasure.

Malcom shifted in his seat, a slight movement away from his uncle's reach. Malcom remembered the first time Bob had cuffed him, when, at age four, he had fingered chocolate frosting on a cake his grandmother had placed on the table. The temptation was too rich, rich like the frosting. It had only been a dab, smaller than a chocolate chip. Malcom had landed on the floor, his head banging up against the sideboard where the dishes rattled when he hit. He had not seen his uncle coming. He was there instantly. Since then, he tried to move away whenever he sensed anger.

Dena and Vera never noticed the tension. Could they not hear the guineas?

Grandma Geslar intervened. "Isn't it strange for a cottonmouth to be away up here? I thought they only lived in the South."

Malcom looked up from his plate. Bob looked at Malcom. "Well, smarty, what you got to say about that?" Bob asked.

Malcom turned his eyes downward, shyly.

Dena and Vera held their forks aloft, food in limbo between their plates and their taste-bud heavens.

"Have you read something about them, Malcom?" Grandma Geslar asked.

"Uh huh," Malcom affirmed. "Cottonmouths usually only go as far this way as Southeast Nebraska. Most the time not."

"How you figure this one got here?" Bob asked.

"I dunno. It maybe came up the Missouri River too far, and followed the Elkhorn over here."

"Damned long way for a snake to crawl." Bob's animosity was visible.

Vera said, "I betcha it was borned up here, and that its family came northward a bit at a time, kind of like Grandma and Grandpa Haskins did from the Ozarks."

"What the hell you saying?" Bob commanded. He clutched his fork in his hand, and the fist of hand and fork sat solid on the table. He was a devil with a stainless steel trident. "You think they come in a covered wagon, all together?"

"No," Vera said, "but its parents or its parents' parents might have come this way over a number of years—like a migration."

"I don't know anything about that. But, I do know this: children should be seen and not heard. You're making me lose my appetite." He pointed his fork tines Malcom's direction. Before anything else was said, the phone rang. Grandma Geslar rose to answer it.

"Yallow," she said. A pause. "Oh, Irene, how are you?"

It was Malcom's mother, calling from the state college where she attended summer teacher-certification classes. Occasionally, she would call to see what trouble Malcom had been to her mother and siblings. He was never allowed to talk to his parents when they called. Bob had said that only people who paid bills should be allowed the privilege of the phone.

"No, no, he's just fine, sitting here and eating supper. He had himself a scare, today, though. A great big cottonmouth surprised him at the front gate, but Bob come and killed it."

Malcom could tell from his grandmother's interjections that his mother was worried about him. Grandma Geslar kept assuring her everything was fine, no one had gotten bit. "Irene, think—if Malcom had been, he'd a been sick unto death by now."

The *put-sput-put* of his uncle's tractor brought Malcom's eyes open, and, as the gate swung back and forth on its hinges, air about Malcom's head, he heard the scree the hinges made, like a hawk flying overhead, like guineas as they fell to sleep on their roosts. It took a moment for Malcom's eyes to clear away the red, and, soon enough, he saw the tractor in the yard, stopped by the gas barrels. His uncle climbed down, pulled his cap off his head, and used it to slap the dust away from his overalls.

Earlier that morning, Bob had come into the living room and awakened Malcom as he slept on the sofa. He asked the boy if he wanted to go into Creighton to the pool hall that afternoon. Even half-asleep, Malcom knew the answer: "Yes." He could forgive Bob's temper, his unfairness, if and whenever he was asked to come along to the pool hall.

A favorite thing, something he had done a thousand times over the last eight summers. Bob was a lazy farmer—he typically worked from sunup to noon, and spent the rest of his day shooting snooker at Gene's Pool Hall or the bull at the Farmer's Union. On rare occasions, he fished Bazile Creek or Grove Lake, sometimes napped long hours in the cool back bedroom. Bob found laziness easy: his mother's farmplace was small—60 acres of dry land. Mostly hay meadow, some corn, some oats, few cattle, fewer hogs. All the poultry, all the gardening belonged to his mother and sisters. Bob often told his story during their trips to town or when they walked corn rows, detasseling:

"I met a Filipino woman during the war," Bob told him. "She wanted to get married and come back to the States. Her name was Hong Villaytong. I called her Villie. I wrote Mom and Dad about her, but they told me I wouldn't have a place to come home to."

"Why did they say that?" Malcom had wondered.

"It wasn't so much Mom. But Dad, he was different. He didn't like the idea of having a foreigner in the family, especially slit-eyed and dark."

"Did you love her?" Malcom asked.

"Didn't matter if I did. Wouldn'ta been right. You have to listen to your folks. Supposed to be that way. Jesus, though, she was sure purty."

Bob puzzled Malcom. How could love not matter? Young as he was, he had read enough, dreamed and fancied enough—believed enough, to know that love was one of the few good things. Granted, love created its own pain, but its jagged pill could also numb it. If he could see it, how could someone Bob's age not? Had he been Bob, he would have defied and brought the woman home. Piss on the family.

When they sometimes sat in a circle of oscillating fans at the Farmer's Union, Bob told Al Wiggert how much he hated farming. Malcom hung upon those negative words and upon the symphony of the airmachine that Cecil Wentz used in the garage to break down tires from their wheels: the explosion, the hiss of escaping air.

"When I came back in '45, I had a chance to work for the Soil Conservation. You remember my brother-in-law? Willie had it all lined up for me. I was ready to start, but Dad, he said no—he needed me on the farm. Shit, the dust gets so bad I can't breathe. There's no money in it. My sisters' teaching pays the bills, and Mom's garden pretty much keeps us fed."

"Your dad's been dead, what, eight years? Why don't you let the place go?" Wiggert asked once.

"Mom wants to stay. See, during the Great Depression, Dad had us

171

two places—this one and a really nice one over to Winnetoon. He had to sell the better place just to keep this one. It's family. You gotta hang on to what's yours."

"Well, dammit, this job ain't so great a one neither," Wiggert remarked. "But it's a living and something to do. Not such a bad place to be, considering." He dug into his shirt pocket, pulled out a Camel and a pack of matches, and lit a smoke. "Want one?" he asked Malcom. Both men laughed, and Malcom grinned.

He never said much to his uncle's friends. He never had to. He was certain, too, his uncle would not have appreciated sharing much of any conversation. Anything was a privilege Bob could too easily revoke.

Just days before, early in the morning, Malcom had climbed the stack of haybales, big as a house, near the barn. On one side, the bales made a staircase upward to a flat top where Malcom lay watching the clouds move overhead, migratory white birds. They moved and moved, moved—there was no weight there, and he felt as if he were floating downstream. He closed his eyes. He listened: the grunting of hogs, the bang and pop of hogfeeder lids; cattle humming in the shade of Grandma Geslar's apple orchard; the meadlowlark, the mockingbird answering.

"What the hell you doing up here?" a gruff voice said.

Malcom flew upright, standing to face his uncle whose face was stone.

"I don't want you on top of this haystack," Bob yelled.

"But—"

"There ain't no buts. Get the hell off my stack!"

"But—"

"No!"

"I always come up here. You never cared—"

"No!"

Malcom moved to the stack's edge to begin his descent. There, two bales he had not remembered hanging so precariously slipped from under his feet. They fell, with him, ten feet to the ground.

Bob stood atop the stack, glaring downward where Malcom lay, sprawled over the bales. "You dead?" he asked.

Maclcom shook his head.

"Then get them goddamned bales back to the top where they were."

One by one, Malcom pulled and dragged the bales upward. They were heavy, nearly eighty pounds, when they were dry. These were still saturated from the morning's dew.

When he was finished, tugging, pulling, grunting, Malcom was scratched and itchy; he sweated like a glass of iced tea. His uncle hovered near, hands fisted at his sides, that uncle-sneer on his face. "Now put them back on the ground. I didn't want them up here in the first place."

Malcom pursed his lips together, and, behind their closure, gritted his teeth hard, so hard his jaws ached with it. Pulling up the first bale, he rolled it to the stack's edge and prepared to drop it.

"No, you don't," Bob commanded. "Carry it down."

Malcom stared dead at his uncle, turned, as if to carry the bale, but let it drop. "Oops," Malcom said. The bale dropped, the twine-binding snapped, and it broke open on the ground.

"Oops, my ass, you goddamned brat," Bob said. "What am I supposed to do with that broken bale?"

"Feed it to the cows," Malcom retorted. "You always break the bales before you do."

He began to walk off, heading down the bale staircase. His uncle grabbed his arm.

"You got a bale to go. Now, get busy, and do it right."

Malcom pulled away. "You told me to bring it up, and I did. I put it back. If you want it somewhere else, now, it's your job." Malcom nearly leapt down the stack and ran toward the house. He heard his uncle yell after him:

"You wanna live to see fifteen? I'll kill you, you piece of dog turd!"

Malcom went to the refuge of his aunts and grandmother. Bob might spank him or slap him in their proximity, but he would never hurt him if they were near. When he told Grandma Geslar what had happened, she said, "Don't worry about Bob. He's just not feeling good. Every time he sprays the fields for bugs, he gets to feeling bad. He'll be okay. You wait and see."

Vera, who was reading True Story romances on the sofa, looked up. "Knothead," she said to Malcom, "it might be best just to stay out of his way."

"I think I'd like to go home to Ord and stay with Dad if he'd let me."

"But you've always stayed every summer," Dena said, shocked.

"You know how Bob says, 'Good to see you go,' when I leave at the end of summer? I think he'd like to see me go already. I think my welcome's worn out."

"Poop," Dena said. "Bob likes having you here."

Malcom shut the memory away just as Bob reached the gate, which Malcom opened for him. Bob would go into the house, wash-up quickly, and be ready to head to town. The boy figured one of the women had spoken to Bob. He figured this was why Bob asked him to go along.

173

"You ready to go?" Bob asked, as he walked by.

"Yes."

"Get over to the pickup and wait for me."

Malcom did as instructed, and sat on the pickup's running board. It would take Bob at least fifteen minutes to do what little he needed to do: Lava the hands, grit his teeth at the mirror to see if they were scummed with mucous and dirt and, if they were a lot, a cursory brushing with an index finger; he would have a cup of coffee tinged with Old Crow; and scour his dresser top for loose change.

When Bob came out the front door, Malcom got into the pickup. Shortly, Bob was in, too.

As they drove down the graveled road toward the highway that led into town, Malcom watched the shelter belts and ragged fence-lines, looking for birds and deer. He enjoyed the ride to town, though nothing ever changed—always the same fence posts, the same bridges, the same ditch water backed up from Bazile Creek, the same silos, barns, wind-mills, and, while they might have moved and shifted a little, the same white-faces on the grazing cattle. There was a security in this sameness, though--something unalterable, permanent, and pleasant in that persis-tency. Here was something consistent he never had to question, never had to ask for. He looked off a distance, where a railroad track ran through the middle of a field, to see if a train was there: there was not, but when there was it was always short—an engine, two or three box cars hauling livestock, a flat car hauling lumber to the Creighton Lumber Yard where his cousin Barney worked, and a caboose.

Malcom thought he might see if he could walk over to Barney's house to visit; Barney had three daughters about his age—Jeanette, Millie and Karen. Jeanette had been his favorite playmate since they were little. Now and then, on slow days at the pool hall, Bob let Malcom walk the four blocks to Barney's, and the two kids would play ping pong in the basement.

"I know what you're thinking," Bob said, interrupting the daydream, the sleepy heat, the wind through the window. The breech of silence shook Malcom awake. His heart jumped, a guinea-leap.

"What?" Malcom asked, wondering what he meant.

"You're wondering why I had you drag those bales back up and then told you I wanted them down."

Malcom said nothing. Truly, he had not given it any thought since he left the farm's driveway. Stating otherwise would have been invalida-tion—he feared saying so would ruin the day.

Bob continued. "In this world, you've got to follow rules and do what people in charge of you tell you. Otherwise, things won't work. The farm's my operation, see. It's a job, a business. Things are done at certain times of the day, and if they don't get done they don't get done. You follow?" Bob looked at Malcom, and, while Malcom was not certain where his uncle was heading with this conversation, he nodded. "So, see, I told you not to play on the stack because the world doesn't allow for time off to play. When the bales fell down, since I'm still in charge of you, I told you to put back what you knocked over. I wanted to see if you could follow orders."

"Why'd you want me to put them back on the ground, afterwards?" Malcom questioned, taking a chance.

"When someone's in charge, you don't ask questions all the time. We had this saying in the war, 'Ours is not to question why. Ours is but to do and die.' Yep, 'do and die.'" Bob sat there, gazing dreamily down the road. The elms on both sides of the ditches raised their arms, like prisoners of war, and made a canopy above the graveled way. Bob wore a self-satisfied grin on his face.

"Not everything makes sense," Bob said. "When I was in boot camp in San Diego, I was put on guard duty outside an ammunitions building. Sergeant told me not to let anyone in without authorization. He gave me an unloaded rifle because the privates couldn't have loaded weapons. Now, figure this: I'm supposed to guard a building, the Japs are off the coast in submarines, and I got no bullets in my gun. They were afraid we'd shoot the wrong person, like I can't tell a slant-eyed Jap from one of us. Hell, it's raining, and I'm getting soaked, but I'm guarding this building. Along comes a second lieutenant in a jeep driven by some M.P. The second lewey gets out and comes up to me. 'Stand down, soldier,' he says. 'I'm going in.' I says, 'No, sir, not unless you have orders.' 'I don't need orders,' he says. 'I'll have you put in the brig,' he says, 'for disobeying my orders.' 'I can't let you, sir,' I told him. 'How you gonna stop me if I want to?' he says next. See, he's starting to piss me off. I held out my rifle and said, 'I have this.' The lieutenant laughed at me. It's raining shit all over us, and he's laughing. He says, 'How's that gonna stop me. They don't issue any bullets to you privates.' 'Maybe not,' I told him, 'but the gun makes one helluva club. I'll cave your head in if you try to pass.'" Bob laughed at the memory.

"Did you get in trouble? Wasn't he giving you orders, too?"

"Yeah, but see, that's the thing: he wasn't in control of me, my sergeant was. If he wanted to tell the sergeant to do something, that was okay, but he couldn't change the sergeant's orders for me. Even if he had rank."

"So you don't have to answer to the higher rank?"

"Well, you do, when you haven't got other orders or when those orders have been changed."

"How'd you know they weren't changed?"

"You gotta trust your instinct." When the two arrived at the highway, Bob slowed at the stop sign just long enough to see no traffic was approaching from his left and pulled onto the blacktop. Bob put his hand out his window and let it glide in the air. Malcom did the same, and, for a few seconds, they were joined in the similar activity of flight, yet how differently they flew. Bob believed he had made a solid argument for duty, obedience, behavior, and Malcom stumbled on the inconsistencies: things on schedule and no time for play, rank but no higher rank, do what you're told but act according to instinct. Bob's hand flew erratically, up and down, trying to catch air but not—a crop duster in trouble. Malcom's hand was steady, cutting the flow, diving through it like a hawk plunging toward the grass-hidden rodent.

"You're gettin' big, now," Bob said, looking seriously at his nephew. "You been laid, yet?"

The look Malcom shot back at him made his uncle laugh again. What was this? An attempt to gain camaraderie? An attempt to extract incriminating information? Malcom could not trust it—his instincts told him not to.

"Well, then, I guess you're still a cherry-boy. You know what that is?"

"Yeah," Malcom said, and he blushed, angrily.

"So, you ever been to first base? Second? Third?"

"Depends on what makes the bases. What are your game rules?" Malcom knew he was heading for trouble. He was the sparrow singing before the jaws of the snake. Yet, he understood hypnosis was a trick. The bird did not have to get eaten, and he could go into the trance of the conversation as far as he chose. There was a danger there, but the quick bird could always fly off.

"Home is score. You ain't scored till you got your dick shellacked. Third is hands inside the underwear. Second is…"

"Third. I've been to third."

His uncle looked shocked. The pickup moved swiftly down the curving highway toward town, the Creighton water tower visible in the near distance. Someone had scaled the tower's ladder. In huge red letters, *Class of '69 has Hair!* made its bold proclamation.

"The hell, you say." Malcom noticed how his uncle bit upon one side of his lip.

"Last summer, after I went home, this girl named Patty Valla and I were playing tag in the pool. I went to tag her and accidentally grabbed her—"

"On the tits?"

"Yeah. She didn't mind. So it happened a little more, not on accident. Then, in the corner of the pool, she let me touch her under the top and in the bottoms."

"She have hair?"

"Well, yeah, of course." Malcom's answer did not seem to please his uncle. Bob scowled and stared at the road ahead of him.

When they hit city limits on Main Street, the two drove past the railroad yard where four deteriorating boxcars sat on a side-rail. Just past the cars, along a creek bank, Malcom saw Bill Cannon's place, a group of old sheds and a rundown house that belonged to his dad's old friend. There was Bill, crawling through one of his pigeon coops, rummaging among the pouters and fantails. That Cannon was still alive surprised Malcom. Surely, his father would have heard he was not, but the previous winter when he had last seen the old man, Bill was very nearly dead. He suffered a spell, had fallen down in the kitchen, hitting his head on a hot cookstove. His ear melted off. Malcom and his dad stood at Bill's bedside, while his wife Mimi, a stoop-shouldered, wrinkled crone with waist-length white hair, moved incessantly behind them. She scooted chairs around the can-littered floor, pushed filthy plates across the table-top, and jabbered: "Doc says Bill had a stroke. Doc says he might die. He won't hear nothing out of that ear no more." She pointed to the place on the stove where he had hit. "His ear stuck to it for a long time, but it finally cooked off. Doc thinks we oughta get to a rest home." She held herself quiet for a moment, her eyes all over her husband, an eyebrow arched. She spoke again: "Bill's the only man I know can look at a young bird's butt and tell its sex. No one can do that but him. Doc says he's gonna have to get rid of his birds. Stroke don't kill him, that will."

Bill lay in his bed, eyes opened, and smiled. He spoke to her, almost inaudibly, "Naw, now, Doc don't know much of nothing."

Here was the proof of it. The old man in the fly pen, Mimi in the garden, scratching out the weeds with a hoe. Authority had spoken outside authority.

Malcom and his uncle continued down the street, past Sloan's Cremery and Hatchery, Manion's Drug, George's Clothing, and the three town taverns. It seemed to Malcom that most of the cars, as few as they

177

were, were parked within short distances of the watering holes; otherwise, in the heat of Nebraska summer, the town was desert. When Bob pulled into a parking space in front of Gene's Pool Hall, Malcom was relieved to arrive. Amazingly, Bob had not said anything the last several miles. If they could get into the pool hall, he might not say anything at all.

Still, too much to hope for. Before Malcom could open the pickup door, Bob grabbed his shoulder. "What you been saying, I hope is a story like kids tell. If what you say is true, you're gonna get your ass in trouble. That girl'll get pregnant, yell rape, something. You keep your hands to yourself and your pecker in your pants."

Pretty much what Malcom had expected. You put rope within a thief's grasp, he steals it, and you hang him with the rope. This is what Bob had done to him.

"It was just a story," Malcom said, and grinned big, all teeth. "I thought you'd like the joke."

"Damned kid," Bob said, shaking his head. The man opened up his pickup door, crawled out, and stepped up the curb. In seconds, he had crossed the sidewalk, pulled open the pool hall's screen door, and entered. Malcom followed, slowly. The pool hall was a sanctuary. Bob would not ridicule him too openly, there, nor say things that might lead to his own embarrassment among friends. He knew he might expect a few jabs, meant in mean jest, but there would be no public accusations, no judgments, no harsh words. Gene Balleweg and his father Otto never allowed cursing in their pool hall; those who did were asked to leave until they could better behave themselves. Otto had tacked posters on the walls: "No Boisterous Language, No Profanity." He could take refuge in that, if nowhere else.

Malcom entered and cigar and cigarette smoke engulfed him. It was a good smell—Switzers and Lucky Strikes, and the pool hall held a good warmth. Summer heat made vapor of the cars parked on Main Street, and Otto's old dog Bumper lay dead asleep in front of a box fan that shivered at the open back door. One of the old men stood at the Coke machine, holding the bottle door open, letting the cool air wave over him.

Bob was already racking balls for snooker. Gene Balleweg sat at a workbench in the pool hall's corner, laboring with a broken television set: transistor tubes and wires lay spread across the bench top. Otto swept cigarette butts off the floor.

Bob stooped for the break, let his cue glide softly, smoothly over his fingers, back and forth, toward the cue ball, away, toward, away, and then the white ball rolled with a pop against the racked balls which zigged and zagged across the table top. Nothing dropped. Bill Ziegler came to the table, his cue in hand, to look the lay over.

"Hey, Gene," Bob said. "Malcom's going to be playing pool one of these days with us big boys."

Gene looked up. "Oh, yeah? How old you, Malcom?"

"Fourteen," the boy answered, and took a seat on a wooden bench at the wall.

"Well, you got a year to wait," Gene said, and focused upon the television repairs. "Gotta be fifteen to play here."

"You know, Gene," Bob continued, waiting his next shot—Bill had just taken three in a row. "I betcha Malcom here knows more about pool and snooker than nearly anyone in here. He's been coming with me since he was in kindergarten, every summer."

"That's a fact," Gene said, without taking his eyes from the transistor he was working to replace. Otto stopped sweeping for a second, looking up. Otto never said much of anything—he was an old man, with sense enough to be quiet. Malcom knew Bob was preparing for a shot; he thought Otto knew it, too.

"Not only that, but I betcha Malcom here knows more about poontang than any single man in here, too."

"That a fact?"

"That's what he tells me." All the men laughed. Bob held his cue in front of him, the tip in front of his face, and chalked it. "Yessir, a young bull in a pasture full of heifers."

More laughter. Malcom's face grew hot. He knew he was blushing. He sat looking at the floor, and, believing laughter might take the edge off Bob's joke, he laughed along, though there was no spirit to his laugh.

"That reminds me of a joke," Bob announced, stooping to make a shot, dropping a ball into a corner pocket. "There was this young bull and an old bull sitting on top of a hill above a pasture, and a hundred young heifers down below them. The young bull was all excited. He got a stiffy long as this cue stick. He says to the old bull, 'Let's run down the hill and get us one of them heifers.' Old bull says, 'Let's walk down and get them all.'" Bob set up for another shot. "You remember that, Malcom."

Otto began sweeping again. "You ought to leave the pup alone," he said. "He's a good kid, quieter than nearly any kid who comes in here, including you big boys."

Malcom stood up from his seat and walked over to where Bumper was sleeping. He stood over the animal and watched it breathe, in, out, slowly. Bumper's upper lip quivered as a fly set there for a second, and then settled into dead stillness again. Otto came over to Malcom. "He's tired," Malcom said.

"Yeah, the heat gets him down, like it does all of us old-timers. He doesn't move much at all anymore."

"He used to play with an old sock. I remember throwing it to him, and he'd go and go."

"Oh, he still does that some, but he plays out quicker than he used to. He was a lot younger when you first started coming here."

"Dogs get old fast," Malcom said, matter-of-fact.

"So do people, in their own way," Otto said, then walked over to the stairwell to go down to the basement where the old Germans played cards, cooing their language. Malcom wandered to the pool hall's front and watched out the window as an occasional car or pickup crawled up and down Main. The sun was a knife, a flat-headed hoe. It cut everything.

Across the street, coming out of the Five and Dime, Malcom saw his cousin, Jeanette, blonde as the sun was yellow. She wore a sleeveless white shirt and white knit shorts that seemed, somehow, too short for Creighton. So much blonde, Malcom could not take his eyes from her. She was a year older than he was. He had not seen, nor talked to her, for a long time—perhaps it was the New Year's Eve card party at his Great Aunt Blanche's, or at a family funeral. He could not recall. He remembered, though, how shy he was around her, a shyness he had never experienced with her before. She had become so much more than the tomboy he used to play hide and seek with in the trees at Grandma Geslar's, more than the best friend who swung with him on a tire swing.

She had come, as girls do, into maturity first. Roundness complemented her, and she carried it confidently down the sidewalk into Manion's Drug Store where, Malcom imagined, she was buying a fountain Coke to cool herself. She had been the object of his imagination often, his shyness compounding itself in ways that, where he could not approach her in the heat of the real world, where serpentine vapors made mirages of everything, he could arise heroically to kiss her lips, to lose his hands in the blondness of her hair, to scorch his hands on the blaze of her skin. And, with such thoughts came also regret.

She had been curious, first, about the distinctions. She was twelve, he was eleven. The family had gathered at the family homestead, owned by their great-great Uncle Bill, and, as always, they left the family to run the trees, to explore the creek bed for fossils and arrowheads. Sitting on the creek bank with their feet in the water, Jeanette kicked water into Malcom's lap. "Oh," she said, "You wet yourself."

Malcom retaliated, standing up in the shallow water, and, with hands and arms working like a well pump, he drenched her. She was not mad, but sat there, her shirt clinging to her skin, which shone pink beneath, and, there, Malcom also saw the first definition of roundness. He sat down beside her, and the two laughed at their mutual wetness.

"You know what?" she said.

"What?"

"The neighbor boy, Teddy Holland—he came over last week and rang the doorbell. When I answered, he said to me, 'Janie ain't got no peter like I do.'"

No girl had ever talked about such things to him before. "Oh?" he answered. "He really said that?"

"Yeah. And then we went to the basement to play ping pong, but actually he showed me it and I got to touch it. It felt funny but nice, too. I didn't know boys could stand up to pee. I thought they had to sit like we do."

"You saw him do that, too?"

"Yeah. It was funny."

"What'd you do?"

"What do you mean?"

"Did you show him anything?"

"He wanted me to, but I didn't. I think it made him mad. He hasn't been back over."

The two of them sat on the creek bank, their feet submerged, their toes digging into the fine sand at the creek bottom. The water was cool and warm, both worlds slipping over their feet and the sensations moving upward, through their legs, up their backs, into their sun-flushed faces. "Teddy told me he's seen some that were two feet long." She held her hands up before her, measuring an approximate distance, like someone illustrating a fish story. "That's big! His wasn't very big at all."

"He's lying."

"Why?"

"I dunno. I've seen grown-up men and guys, in the swimming pool dressing room. What I've seen isn't all that big. Not even a foot."

"How big is yours?" she asked.

"I'm just a kid, still," was Malcom's answer.

"Oh." She sat silent and her toes came up, peeking above the water. He noticed she had painted her toenails pink. He moved a foot over to touch hers, making it seem an accident.

"Do you wanna see?" she asked. He felt jitters rising from his stomach to his chest—butterflies, his mother would have called them—and an instantaneous leap in his groin. He was about to say *yes* when Jeanette's sisters popped over the rise behind them, surprising them both.

"It's lunch time," Karen called. "We're wanted back to the house."

Nothing ever occurred, after that. Malcom thought about it often. He wondered if Jeanette did. He was curious, he was wholly curious, and yet she was a cousin, distant enough not to be family but still family. He wished, and he did not wish.

Malcom saw Jeanette come out of the drug store. He wanted to see her again, to talk to her, to walk with her. He turned from the window and saw his uncle rising from a pool shot he had missed. "Can I go for a walk?" he asked, careful not to specify what he really wanted. He had once told his uncle about the near occurrence. His uncle had dismissed it.

"A peep show, huh?" he had said. "She was just being snoopy. Be glad you didn't take the bait."

Now, though, Bob's mind on the game, having not seen the girl across the street, he gave his permission for Malcom to leave. Malcom walked slowly out of the pool hall, trying to portray calm, trying not to draw attention to himself, and, once the door slapped shut behind him, he quickened his pace so as to place himself a half block behind Jeanette.

There, he watched the sway of her hips, the steady slap, slap of her sandaled feet. His mind turned over and over the creekside conversation, and he created conclusions to the scenario had her sisters not arrived. What, truly, would he have known to do? Wet behind the ears. Pup. This is what Bob would have said. Cherry boy. Dimple dick. No lead in the pencil--oh, but there was lead.

Jeanette must have sensed she was being followed. Now and then, she would slow, turn slightly to look behind her, and Malcom would duck behind a tree or turn his back so she could not tell it was him. He wondered where she was going. She was walking toward the park, not toward her house.

A plane flew overhead, and Malcom looked up to watch its vapor trail. He kept walking as he watched, his feet finding their way down the cement. When he put his eyes back to where Jeanette should have been, he found she had disappeared. He kept on, and, after a distance, Jeanette jumped at him from behind a tree. " Boo!" she yelled.

Malcom felt himself go white, his heart throb, his knees go rubber. She laughed and grabbed hold of one his shoulders to shake him. "How come you followed me so far?" she asked. "I kept wondering when you'd catch up."

"I dunno," he said. "I thought maybe you might not want to be bothered. You were busy going someplace."

"I'm not that busy," she said.

"Where you going?"

"To the pool. You wanna come swimming?"

"I can't," he answered. "I never brought my trunks with me, and Bob probably wouldn't let me anyway."

"Well," she said. "Come walk me to the pool and watch me."

Malcom nodded his assent. The two walked onward, down the sidewalk into the tree-shaded park. In the distance, they could hear the kids whooping and hollering, screaming, the sound of water splashing and of the diving board banging. "How long have you been here?" Jeanette asked.

"For a couple of weeks already."

"How come you didn't come see me?"

"I don't get to town very much, and Bob doesn't like me to go anywhere."

"That sucks," she said. Her use of the word amused him. It was a word he and his buddies used, back home, and it was a word he enjoyed hearing her say.

"Yeah, it really does. I don't like being here this summer."

"Why not?"

"Bob seems mad all the time."

When they arrived at the pool's entrance, Jeanette said, "I'm going in, but you can sit on the bleachers outside the fence and watch. I'll come over and talk to you."

Malcom moved to the bleachers, sat on the lowest bench, nearest the fence, and waited for Jeanette to emerge from the pool shower room. When she came out, she was wearing a white two-piece suit, and her hair and back were lightly wet, glistening, from the pre-pool shower. She walked on the far side of the pool, one bare foot steady in front of the other, and her legs—from toe to knee to thigh—synchronized into the roundness of her hips. She was such beautiful whiteness, the snow would seem filthy by comparison, the moon a black eye. She waved at him, and his eyes followed the raised arm downward to the arm socket, the soft pit there, across the collar bone, to her white roundness. He felt the ache in his center.

Up and up she crawled the ladder of the high board. Steadily, she approached the board's end. Then, she plunged off, the board snapping her upward, and down she came, her right leg tucked under her arms into a can opener. When she hit the water, it flew up and splattered him. She had made a perfect leap, and he was wearing it.

She came out of the water, the cups of her top sagging as she bent forward, and he was certain he saw a nipple. As she stood, she kicked the water off her legs in his direction. The droplets hit him like sparks. "Did I get you?" she asked. She could see the obvious.

"Yes," he said. "That was a good can opener."

"You think that was good, watch this." She hurried away, her steps quick, her hips moving back and forth like an up-tempo metronome. Climb after climb, leap after leap, Jeanette entertained Malcom. First, came a back flip in pike position, the whole length of her floating downward, an angel tumbling. Next, a gainer. Next, a cartwheel off the board's end. Next, and most thrilling, a leap into a split. And, every time, as she came out of the water, that little bit of cleavage, that most precious display of white, that most wonderful sparkling of water-speckled skin. The suit she was wearing seemed less white, more skin. Soon, he imagined he could see her through the material. His eyes imaged everything.

"I've been taking diving lessons," she announced.

"You're good," he said. "I learned how on my own."

"I wish I could see you," she said, meaning his dives. His thoughts turned it to something else, that previous time, creekside.

Suddenly, the sound of guineas magnified: the City Hall siren called the Volunteer Fire Department to some emergency. Malcom knew that Gene Balleweg would close shop to run to the fire and that Bob would have no idea where he was.

"I better go," he said. "Bob'll be wanting to get to the farm." He rose from the bleachers, rubbed his hands on his pants as if to rub a soreness away.

"Next time you come, come see me."

"Okay," Malcom said. "But I think maybe I'll ask Dad if I can come home early. I don't want to stay on the farm anymore."

"Well, if you do come, you know—"

"Yeah." He looked at her, wet and gleaming, one last time, and her eyes seemed sad in the knowledge of the inevitable. They would never be close again. This was the last occasion for such play. Life was going to become serious too quickly. They had come to the edge of their diving boards to fly like swans, teetered on their tiptoes, arms uplifted as if to reach something just beyond their fingertips. The springing end of youth and the submissive fall into adulthood.

Malcom ran from the pool, up the sidewalk that led to the park's entrance. He could hear the ambulance and fire truck sirens in the distance.

He wondered where Bob would be. All along Main, Malcom ran down the sidewalk, past his Great Uncle Elmer's house where the old man sat on a porch swing, waiting to see if the trucks would come by his place. Elmer never saw Malcom, nor would he have known the boy had he seen him. He ran past the drive-in where high school kids in hopped-up cars played Beatles or Rolling Stones music, drank their root beer floats or licked their cones. One young man had very long hair, a pair of ragged blue jeans with a patch of American flag on the rump. The girl who was with him Malcom recognized as Trudee Tepner, daughter of the Chevy dealer; she had braided hair and pink sunglasses. He ran past Hengstler's Funeral Chapel, where a sign in the window advertised the forthcoming rites for one of the city's matrons, Mrs. Katie Maute. And on he ran, toward the pool hall where his uncle's pickup should have been parked. It was not there.

He slowed his run. He slowed it to a walk. He breathed heavily, longingly, taking in air. "I'm in deep shit," he said to himself. Sweat rolled down his forehead, stinging his eyes, and coursed down his cheeks, dripping from his chin. It ran down the sides of his rib cage, under his shirt, and felt cool. He heard a motor accelerating behind him, coming quickly down the street. He thought, at first, it might be one of the volunteers rushing to the fire station, but when he turned he saw it was Bob's pickup. Bob honked the horn, aimed the pickup toward him, and cut across the street's center lane. He brought the pickup to a screeching, skidding halt. The driver's side front wheel ran up over the curb and Malcom jumped back toward the dress shop behind him.

"What the hell you been doing?"

"I went for a walk, like I asked."

"Where the hell you walk to? I been looking all over for you."

Malcom stammered. "I-I met up with Jeanette and walked her to the swimming pool."

"Goddamned kid. I mighta figured something like that. Get in the pickup."

Malcom obeyed, and, for the better part of the ride to the farm, Malcom endured Bob's lecture: "You tell me exactly where you're going, or you're not going to town with me ever again." "When that whistle blew, how was I to know it wasn't you hurt?" "That whistle was for a grass fire. What if that fire had been on my place, and I needed to get home? What would you have done? How the hell would I have found you?" "Why you want to mess with Jeanette for? She's your cousin, no matter how distant." "I oughta slap you around to wake you up."

185

Malcom was careful not to commit. Statements during inquisitions never free the prisoner; they merely expedite the execution. Bob held his severed head already, Malcom knew it. Further drawing and quartering would avail nothing, even if his defense made sense. The phoenix rose out of its own ash, not from parts. He needed to go through the fire, as best he could. And the guineas— they flew into the trees and chattered, out of reach. He was not in any position to fly, yet. His chattering would have to wait just a little longer.

Bob turned onto the gravel road that would lead the last five miles to the farm. He had, somehow, expended all his energies and regrouped in quiet. He seemed frustrated. Was it from Malcom's failure to engage? Finally, Bob spoke: "What do you have to say for yourself?"

Dust rose behind the pickup, its smell sweet. An adjacent field had been mowed, and new, green bales sat in intervals, sunning themselves like snakes did. A meadowlark sat on a post, whistling. Malcom said, "I'm sorry. It won't happen again." He knew he meant what he said. The words were genuine, as true as the grass in the meadow, the sun, the dust, the birds. Bob would never know such genuineness.

Bob brought the pickup to a stop at the Bazile Creek bridge. "Wanna drive?" he asked.

Malcom said, "I don't know how."

"You might be taught."

Malcom crawled out his pickup door as Bob slid across to the passenger side. The boy walked around the front of the truck, opened the door, and stepped into the cab, slipping his body into the seat, his legs under the steering wheel. Bob leaned back into his corner, put his right arm out his window, working his fist upon the air, squeezing. "Ready?" Bob asked.

"What do I do?"

"You take that gear, there," he said, pointing to the right side of the steering column, "and you pull it forward a bit and down three notches. That'll put you into drive. Be sure you put your foot on the brake, that big pedal on the floor, there."

Malcom did as directed. The pickup did not move.

"Well, you gotta take your stupid foot off the brake. Then, you're ready to go."

Once again, Malcom did as directed, and the pickup started crawling down the roadway.

"You wanna get somewhere? You have to put some gas to it. That's the pedal next to the brake. Put your foot to it."

Malcom could feel his nerves unraveling, like a baseball that had come out of its cover, the protective strings and yarn rolling free, revealing the blue, rubber core. Malcom could see the ditches like canyons on either side of him, and he was determined to keep the pickup in the middle of the gravel. He preferred crawling.

"Give it gas, dammit!" Bob commanded. Malcom did. The pickup lurched forward, and Malcom pulled his foot off. His head and Bob's bounced on their necks, forward, back. "Give it gas easier," Bob commanded again, and, again, the pickup lurched, and the heads jerked. "Jesus Christ," Bob muttered. Malcom kept trying, without his uncle's direction, and soon they were going down the road, but in spurts of fast-slow motion. "Stop the pickup," Bob commanded. Malcom braked but too hard. Again, the heads snapped on their springs. "Put it back into park, just the opposite of how you got it into drive."

Malcom did. "Now get out," his uncle said. His voice had an edge to it. Malcom opened up his pickup door, stepped out, and his uncle slid across the bench seat, back under the wheel. He looked hard at his nephew, and formed his hand into a gun shape, pointing the barrel of his index-finger at the boy's chest. They were just a little more than a mile from Grandma Geslar's. "You walk the rest the way home. You wanted to walk in town—well, walk here. I've had enough of your bullshit. Give you the chance to do things, and you fuck up. You don't stay where you're supposed to in town, and then you act like a retard with my truck. People who are too stupid to do anything else can drive, goddammit. What the hell's wrong with you?"

"I've never driven before," Malcom said. He looked at his shoes, toed the gravel.

"That's pretty damned clear. You didn't have to jerk the thing back and forth. You're supposed to keep the gas even so the truck rolls at a steady speed."

"I did the best I could, and I imagine I'll get better."

"You'll never find out in my truck."

"Why did you ask me to drive?"

"To prove you couldn't. I'll tell your grandma that you're coming along directly. Let's hope she doesn't put away your supper before you get there."

His uncle dropped the pickup into gear, stepped on the gas, and the tires spun in the gravel. Dust engulfed Malcom. It smelled sweet but smothered; in the eyes, it was like a pleasant irritation, an itch that wanted more scratch so itched the more. He began walking, briskly because he was young, briskly because he was free. The elms loomed overhead, still the prisoners of war, still locked in their stationary march down a country lane to a house where vacant people filled their vacant days with vacancy.

Meadowlarks sung and a quail asked its repetitive question, "Bob white?" No, no, no, Bob was not white. He was a darkness, the humus of his own soil where little grew and little worth came out of it what did grow. He was the dark room he napped in, and his dreams, none of them ever coming true, had been stored away like the tools that rusted in the collapsing tool shed. "Bob white?" the quail asked again, and Malcom smiled because he knew such small birds had such small brains. His own brain had been the guinea, its oddity a self-awareness that he flew from, his fears bravery in a treetop. He had not understood, until now, what the treetop was. On his uncle's ground, he was ever looking for the shadow, the polecat, the coyote, the fox, to pounce upon him. Sure, guineas had to fly to survive, and, equally sure, predators prowled their nocturnal habitations to subsist on such odd creatures. Why one species should be weaker than another was a mystery but also a fact of nature. But, in what manner was the predator weak and the guinea strong?

The treetop. Heights and, from those heights, the ability to see—the approach from far off, the distance to which one might fly. The fences, the boundaries over which one might sail effortlessly.

The oddity. The dissimulation of birds. Nothing quite like it, nothing as ugly, nor nothing as special inside its feathers. A bird, but so strange it could draw attention to itself without trying.

Voice. And music. Coyotes could sing, but they had fewer songs than the guinea. A warble, only, not tremolo. Comparatively inarticulate. Coyotes intoned their quavering misery, their night-time aloneness, their one song, their lonely call to the loveless moon. And polecats and foxes—stench and stealth, only. No music but the absence of it, *vox silencia*. The guinea had range, from mute to crescendo, from *vox harmonious* chirps to cacophony. All of it a symphony of existence, *vox populi*.

Bob might as well have bayed futilely at the moon—it, and nothing else, could love him back. Maybe this was why he growled so, this, and because he could not fly.

Malcom knew what he would do. He would grow into manhood, choose to smoke or not, choose to press the gas or kill the motor, choose to shoot or to leave the cue chalkless, choose to love or not, but never choose to let someone, something make his choices. Bob dumped him off to make him walk—he could not make him walk slowly, could not make him walk swiftly. Instinct told him to fly to the heights of his own brain, to voice his displeasure or pleasure as loudly or as silently as he wished, against or in praise of whomever, whatever he chose.

When he got to the farmhouse, he ate his supper without conversation although Bob sat nearby, waiting for a morsel of complaint to fall from his nephew's lips. He left his uncle unsatisfied. Afterward, when Grandma Geslar and her daughters were clearing the table, Malcom cleared his throat. "I want to call my father. I want to go home. I don't need to be here anymore."

His grandmother tried to protest, his aunts scolded, blamed him, and called him thankless and inconsiderate. Bob said, "Good riddance to bad rubbish."

The next day, his father drove the two hours there to pick him up. They ate a lunch of bologna sandwich and iced water. "It's the least we can do," Grandma Geslar said. Father and son knew it almost was.

Then, Malcom was on his way. He would not need to come back any time soon. He listened to the highway hum as his father's car moved forward, and he fell asleep in its lullaby.

PLAIN SENSE

> *. . . all this*
> *Had to be imagined as an inevitable knowledge,*
> *Required, as a necessity requires.*
> --Wallace Stevens, "The Plain Sense of Things"

Plain speech for a plain people:
weather-words gray as old lumber;
old sheds and old houses
sitting on the tilted legs of wind;

verbs the cranes dancing, the snow geese dangling,
something wild dashed
into wilder brush or wood, the slow steady plow
of an idea through black dirt, the blossom.

We drive the long, sleepy phrases, and
turn sharp on a country thought;
the gravel punctuates, the noun-heart steers.

Mark Sanders

A sentence like a pivot: the steel spans circle;

the cold spray a nourishment, a continued green.

*

Two ways of looking at things:

Rain falling into your face from a black sky.
Or, the head turned toward the ground,
the face blurred in the puddle where rain drops.

In the snow funnel, walking blindly through the white of it,
frost in the beard, sweet moist on cold lips.
Or, still: an iced pond, a silver slip of creek.

The mouse in the alfalfa, the hawk's black eye.
Or: the turn, the absolute fall.
The beak, the flesh, the stone talons.

The ground, too, like stone.
Or, the mud temptation.
Or, the porous dark, the quilted bed, the dormant seed.

*

A man wears a sandstone face.
Call it character.
Call it erosion.
The deep cut, the gradual smoothing, the permanence.

*

Every which way the wind:
the cattle-clouds, the skiff-snakes, the gnat-dust;
the dead dressed in green robes swaying, breathing, amorous.

*

Old men passed us bottles of home-brew and we drank.

190

The taste bitter, the spillage dripping from the spigots of our faces.
The bitterness we recall as sweet: it was cold and wet on a parched day.

Old women poured us coffee from granite-wear pots.
Bavarian china chipped or cracked: chapped lips against our lips.
The hot potion we sweetened, clouded with cream or sipped straight
        and black.
The house was a mood: damask, vinegar, alum, dust.

*

The swallow is a question mark, the fence posts exclamations.
The elliptical miles, the emphatic cottonwoods.

*

Today, the tasseled breasts of corn, the bearded milo.
The wheat ambles and jigs; the alfalfa swims nude in a blue-green pond.
How can you doubt the optimism of hail, tornado, drought?

*

A child toes the dust and sees creation.
Someone dead smiles in the cloud.

A child picks up a stone and skims the water top.
More pleasure in plunking it to the depths.

A child dismembers a grasshopper.
Later, he puts it back together to dismember it again.

*

The metaphor went around the property.
Meshed, electric, paneled, barbed.

It sectioned the place like a quilt.
It linked.

The cattle did not wander, the calves bawled and sucked.

Pigs squealed and the feeders banged.
The horses ran or lulled about, nodding.

It made the garden secure.

The city folk who came out to sell us something
had to stop at the gate where a big dog stood, growling,
baring its teeth.

*

A young woman once sat in a pickup truck
high atop a country hill, the hot then cold wind
blowing through open windows, her hair streaming her face,
the black clouds on the night sky
defining blackness.

The music was what she loved: the wind-moan,
the sky-sigh heavy, the cloud heart-knock.
The truck waltzed on its tires.

And best, most best: the sharp light like nerve-something, *yes*,
and, *yes, yes*, the thunder.

*

A plain word is a simple tool.
A nut tightened on its bolt,
the pieces holding.

*

The bull snake crawling on the blacktop
is exact.

The vapor, a heat-thing that crawls and disappears,
is exact.

The meadowlark, perched on a fencepost,
singing, is exact.

And when it flies away, and yet you hear the song,
and feel the heat coil or fly about you,

this is exact, too.

*

It has to have a certain flatness,
like old folks talking on a porch swing
under the bright bulbs of stars,
the electric buzz of cicadas, a chain creaking.
Soft words like the long smoke of a good cigar.

It has to be an observable silence, each spoken stone
compelling,
a flint,
or the snarl of a black cloud-wall just before the point is made.

*

Our eyes hold the almighty sky in callused hands.
Our ears sip deep the odorous blue.

*

The swirl of leaves
is the rattle of brown bones down casket roads.

The swirl of geese and crane,
their bell-gongs,
is trinity: birth, covenant, everlasting.

*

An old farmer danced a polka with a pump handle.
All the old and young cows cried as the music poured.

He switched partners, holding hands with a hay hook,
swinging bales, the dust kicking its heels.

All day like this: everything a tune, everything a dance.
Even as he slept, there was a rhythm to it.

*

There must be a recognition of need,
and need is the plain sense of things near.

*

Out here, water is the great wheel turning.
Listen to the gurgling gears of pond, creek, river.

Out here, we stand at the center of the great wheel,
and we are the ponds, the creeks, the rivers.

So long as there is water, the necessary machine runs.

*

Were the weather any different,
it would not be ours.

Neither the land, how it lifts and falls,
the way a finch dips
or the steep to which the hawk glides
or the depths to which it plunges.
The burdens, the joys, the loves, the broken things:
they would not be ours if they were different.

Anything else and we should destroy the essential:
the gopher-intelligence, the ground muscle,
the harvest-soul.

What is here is ours.
What is here suffices.

The Creighton Pool Hall

The smoke here is friend. The break of the rack
quiet conversation. Along the brown-gray walls,
where wood benches sit in the haze, cue sticks
stand their silent guard. Today no one speaks,
not the old farmers with sun burned dull
on their faces, nor the smart-mouthed kids
who fool with snooker, smoky silence
held in their lungs. Whatever is cool works hard
to stay that way. The squat Coke machine sweats
in its sun-dusted corner. A pin-up selling cement
ashes with age, her wax-smooth body scarred
where someone stubbed out his cigarette.
A box fan shivers at the alley door,
an old dog noses out a space of shadow.

Bladen, Nebraska

"With us it's always a feast or a famine."
—Willa Cather, One of Ours

Store fronts are closed coffins, here,
their pine-boarded windows webbed with dust.
A transient wind blows and hobo-dirt,
crossing a poor man's fields,
leaves upon rails of steel sky.

Stony streets snore beneath wheels
of crawling trucks and tractors pulling discs.
Each week the cars seem fewer, and the souls
who drive these narrow roads are worms
earth-locked in a Mason jar.

It's the dying who stay. Anguished
by the barbs of death and debt, old farmers
are weathered posts. Gravity
pulls the ladies earthward—see them
bent in their gardens, the avalanche of bodies.

Life to all is a slow waltz
around short blocks,
a nodding of heads. It's the shuffle of cards
at the corner tavern, voices murmuring,
the dance of sprightly weeds upon graves.

The Oasis Bar

Leaden light and smoke choke the lounge
in gloomy blue-green hue. Happy hour
is not happy but half-hearted ritual.
Old jokes have no punch. Serious talk
is the murmur of slow-moving fans.

Sometimes, a young farmer or cowboy,
lust-lonely, marches across the dance floor
to meet defeat: the women here are ugly
with toughness. When pairings take,
romance is a sin of omission.

Most folks here are extensions of their chairs,
stiff, still, new moons stuck in phase,
stationary above their planet tables.
The hours shamble away like dollar bills.
Talk is the desultory chink of glass.

When the sad hour comes, when the sad songs
cease their play and everyone leaves,
the night is foul, empty as a bottle.
The moon's face is a blotter,
stained with beer, sopped with smoke.

Sitting on Foth's Roof, with Beer

for Kelly

Dirt hung upon the air like a tan curtain.
The auburn sun, a yolk
on a hot, greased pan of prairie,
popped and darkness oozed.
Sputter of diesel pump.
A yowling dog. Drone of heavy trucks,
far off, on and on, on the blacktop.

"Let's go to the roof," you had said,
to fill idle time with more than talk.
We crawled out an upstairs window,
shinnied up a steep pitch of wood shingles.
Roped the cooler to the chimney
and sat there—nine beers, ten.
In the dark, maples sipped a dark draft.
The leaves chatted and waltzed.

"We're two cans of beer, Bud," you said,
meaning what we had left.
I thought of that stale something in us
drunk, stale-something.
You'd be married in a week,
and I'd be gone.
We're sour mash, friend.
                        I slid down,
left you straddling the peak,
can held high,
toasting the night.

ROY SCHEELE ℬ

Roy Scheele is poet-in-residence and associate professor of English at Doane College in Crete. His poems have been widely published in such journals as *Poetry*, *Prairie Schooner*, and *The Sewanee Review* and in a number of anthologies, including *To the Clear Fountains : 100 American Poems* (The Dolphin Press, 2002). He also has published criticism, as well as interviews with contemporary poets Miroslav Holub, Hayden Carruth, W.R. Moses and W.D. Snodgrass.

ℬ

AT THE DROUGHT'S HEIGHT

All night over a field

at the edge of town,
over the roof of a shed,
the Dipper that's hung

on the nail of the polestar
turns till it's upright,
the drops at its lip
dusty but gleaming,
wetting the sky with its light.

EOHIPPUS

Horse of the Dawn, given free morning rein
to browse here in the sea of waving grass
after the Inland Sea became a plain
and rudimentary mammals came to pass,
I see you now, etched in a lens's glass
at the small end of evolution's scope,
tethered by placidity, not a rope,
grazing contentedly among your kind,
scenting the wind, breaking into a lope,
the future dark and far beyond your mind.

THE HUNTER, HOME

Behind the neighbor's roof, Orion's down,
all but his head and shoulders,
at two a.m. this mild December night.

Three stories' worth of sloping tiles
drawn up like a comforter!
He reaches, on one elbow, for the light.

UNCLE LOU

I remember he kept, when I was young,
a little flock of pigeons in the shed.
I would hear them chortling behind the door
as he fumbled with the latch. We'd enter
a dimness full of the richest smells —

mash and droppings, feathers and sidling dust —
the doorway lying tipped across the floor
in a light in which we stood exalted.

Once he caught one and, while cupping its wings
in his hands, let it peck at the corn
and millet that I held out to it. And that

was like him — to make you a part of things.
Today the flat of my outstretched empty hand
tingled when I heard that he was gone.

Barbara Schmitz &

Poet Barbara Schmitz retired from a long-time teaching position in English at Northeast Community College in Norfolk, Nebraska. She is a former editor of *Elkhorn Review*, and she has had poems published in such journals as *Prairie Schooner*, *Laurel Review*, *Nebraska Review*, *Silverfish Review*, *Poetry Motel*, *Hurakan*, *River Styx*, and *Kansas Quarterly*. Her chapbook, *Making Tracks*, was published by Suburban Wilderness Press in Duluth. She is also the author of *The Lives of the Saints* (Main-Travelled Roads #8, 1996), *How to Get Out of the Body* (Sandhills Press, 1999), *The Upside Down Heart* (Sandhills Press, 2003), and *How Much Our Dancing Has Improved* (Backwaters Press, 2005). A resident of Norfolk, she gives psychic readings in the form of poems and is a winner of the Encouragement Award from the Nebraska Arts Council's Individual Artists Fellowships program (1997).

NOTE FROM SCHMITZ ABOUT SANDHILLS PRESS

For a long time Sandhills was the only press in Nebraska. The press was there recognizing Plains and Nebraska writers before Logan House, Backwaters, and Lone Willow. Sandhills saved my writer's soul. Even though I had lived almost all my life in the Great Plains my writing most often didn't address the same subjects as the majority of Nebraska writers--the land, the landscape. It did not usually include cows, horses, barns, some of the oft-included Nebraska images. I usually wrote about the people of this chunk of the country and often used myself and spiritual inquiry for subject matter. No matter to Sandhills. Mark Sanders offered to publish *The Lives of the Saints*, a somewhat odd collection of "persona" poems exploring the dark side of human nature, and then took on my first full-length collection as well. I had written for many years, felt unseen and unrecognized, realizing I didn't fulfill the usual expectation of a "Nebraska" writer. But, Sandhills brought out my poems nevertheless, bringing attention to my years of effort and adding a different perspective to the Nebraska literary scene.

Sanders often astonished me with his effort and energy. Before a large commemorative Nebraska Writers Festival orchestrated by J.V. Brummels at Wayne, he personally collected and illustrated around fifty different poems, crafting post cards of local writers' work in time for the festival.

Even though Sandhills has moved its locale following the odyssey of editor Sanders, it has been continually present, ferreting out work by Plains writers, bringing it into print in The Main-Traveled Roads series of chapbooks, a rich collection of full length-books, plus special anthologies (i.e., *The Plain Sense of Things*, featuring poems by eight Plains poets). Sandhills Press has shone a light on the life and culture of the Great Plains at the end of the 20th Century and on into the new millennium for readers, writers, and audiences of much more than just this region of America.

℘

SUPPER

I'm making a tuna casserole,
adding white and green noodles
to water boiling in a cast iron pan.
He's fixing the broken boards
in the fence. Our son's off playing.

I resist the urge to go to the back door,
storm glass still on,
and wave a movie wave
across the greening grass, across
the theater, across eternity.

All the couples "forever
and ever, Amen" repeating
this scene, wearing these costumes
complete with opposite sets of genitals
as if they were real, and we existed,
he and I, in this time,
this old house, supper almost ready.

TWO-STEP

We're dancing
My father and me
This isn't the dress

I planned to wear
That one was pink
This one is green but
the pink one tore
when I was washing it

I don't feel very pretty
at this fancy wedding
But my father and I
are shuffling along
He's not good at dancing
I always thought
I could have been
but didn't get dance lessons
and turn to stone
when anyone looks at me

He's shorter

like he is with my mother
We're banging toes
like our lives that only bumped
didn't match smooth
didn't reach deep
into each other's language—
foreign tongues

He'd say *football*
I'd say *poem*
He's smiling
So am I
It's our last
but we don't know

How My Daddy Held Me

Baby girl in bonnet
Fat fat cheeks
Hand in my mouth
I'm staring at the camera
He's in a suit in a tie Big
hand on my baby girl
belly and hip Holding me
Talking something
Talking nice
He never sang
No one in my house did
Open the doors oh loved ones
Let in all the all the
music I look dark
Now I'm blond Already my
legs are long He is
a handsome father White
forehead working hard digging
ditches for the water company
Autumn I imagine
too much foliage for spring
About fifty years ago He wasn't
afraid to touch me then

FLOOD

What's happening to me? she sighs
trying on a polka-dotted dress
in K-Mart's tiny coffin of a dressing room

I look at her humped back
It's called aging I say
We all have to go there
You're showing us the way

She looks down
Her belly droops under her slip

You said it! she says
Just like that!

Does she think she can hold
back the raging water if
she never names it

never says the word flood?

She likes this dress She just
wants to look a little more
She can't see the road signs
as she tries to guide me to Richman Gordman

My dad can't take her
Can't see to drive, only a hole
where the cancer doctor stole
half his blue-eyed treasure

People stare at him she says
Golden years! foam on her lip
Don't believe it!
You're lucky if you die young

STEVEN P. SCHNEIDER ℰↃ

Steven P. Schneider is Professor of English at the University of Texas Pan American. Steven is a founding member of the South Texas Literacy Coalition in the Rio Grande Valley and is the recipient of two Big Read grants from the National Endowment for the Arts.

Steven Schneider has published his poetry widely and given readings throughout the United States, including public performances at the Iowa Summer Writing Festival, the Fort Kearny Writers' Conference, the UTPA Summer Creative Writing Institute, and the South Texas Literary Festival. He has also been interviewed and read his work on NETV. Steven Schneider's poems and essays have been published in national and international journals, including *Critical Quarterly*, *Prairie Schooner*, *Tikkun*, *The Literary Review*, and featured in *American Life in Poetry*.

He is the author of several books, including two collections of poetry, *Prairie Air Show* and *Unexpected Guests*, a scholarly book entitled *A.R. Ammons and the Poetics of Widening Scope* and the editor of *Complexities of Motion: New Essays on A.R. Ammons's Long Poems*. He is a winner of an Anna Davidson Rosenberg Award for Poetry and a Nebraska Arts Council Fellowship.

NOTE FROM SCHNEIDER ABOUT SANDHILLS PRESS

I moved to Kearney, Nebraska from Seattle, Washington, in the summer of 1995 to take a teaching position in American Literature at the University of Nebraska at Kearney (UNK).

How would I discover my place, a Jew raised on the East Coast, among hog farmers, prairie grasses, and buffalo? What would I choose to write about? How would the voice in my poems change? And who would I talk to about the focus of my research on contemporary American poetry?

One of the reasons I decided to come to Nebraska is that the poet Don Welch taught at UNK. Don suggested I attend the Nebraska Writers conference, an annual event that rotated to different campuses around the state. I remember meeting and hearing Ted Kooser and Bill Kloefkorn read at these programs. I also met a variety of other poets who lived and wrote in Nebraska: Twyla Hansen, Barbara Schmitz, Roy Scheele, Nancy McCleery and JV Brummels. I became friendly with Hilda Raz, who taught with me in the Fort Kearny Summer Writers' Conference that I helped to establish at UNK, and who published several of my poems in *Prairie Schooner*.

I met at one of these annual literary conferences the poet, critic, and publisher Mark Sanders. Mark was open and friendly, as were many of the writers and scholars who lived and worked in Nebraska. Perhaps there was a special bond between us because of the sparseness of the landscape and the relatively small number of writers and artists in a state best known for its cattle and beef. At one of these meetings Mark asked me how I was adjusting to life in Nebraska. I told him that I had begun to write poems about places in and around Kearney, like Cotton Mill Lake, the Platte River, and Calamus Reservoir. Several of these poems – "Platte River Liftoff," "Walking Beside Calamus Reservoir," "Sandhills in Late Summer" – later found their way into my chapbook *Prairie Air Show* that Mark published. I have always been grateful for his willingness to embrace a "transplant" and for the commitment of Sandhills Press to publish contemporary poetry. Mark's press has helped to foster the strong sense of community among Nebraska writers.

I am delighted that he has chosen two of my poems, "Prairie Air Show" and "Chanukah Lights Tonight," to feature in this anthology. The first of these poems, about a milkweed pod slowly opening on the prairie, is about the mystery and often unnoticed beauty of the Nebraska landscape. It reflects my attempt to be at home in this place, to be a student of its ways. The second poem, "Chanukah Lights Tonight," expresses what it feels like to light a Chanukah menorah in winter with Christmas lights inside and outside every other home in the neighborhood. Although a poem of exile, it contains within it the celebration of light over darkness and the nostalgia for childhood and home.

℘

CHANUKAH LIGHTS TONIGHT

Our annual prairie Chanukah party-
latkes, kugel, cherry blintzes.
Friends arrive from nearby towns
and dance the twist to "Chanukah Lights Tonight";
spin like a dreidel to a klezmer hit.

The candles flicker in the window.
Outside, ponderosa pines are tied in red bows.
If you squint,
the neighbors' Chrisrmas lights
look like the Omaha skyline.

The smell of oil is in the air.
We drift off to childhood
where we spent our gelt
on baseball cards and matinees,
cream sodas and potato knishes.

No delis in our neighborhood,
only the wind howling over the crushed corn stalks,
Inside, we try to sweep the darkness out,
waiting for the Messiah to knock,
wanting to know if he can join the party.

PRAIRIE AIR SHOW

Just because
      no one sees

the pods
      of the milkweed

slowly open
      on the prairie

on a cold October night
      doesn't mean

we should ignore
       their white silken treasure

readying itself
       for flight

on a sunny afternoon
       when the cottonwoods

are turning gold.
       Who can say

if the prairie dogs.
       sun-bathing

on the hillside
       have come to see

the air show,
       but when a trio

of pods burst open
       and the white silken parachutes

float over the prairie
       meadow

even the sharp green tips
       of the yucca

crane
       in anticipation.

Mary K. Stillwell 𝔈

Mary K. Stillwell is a native of Nebraska. She has studied writing in New York with William Packard, Erica Jong, and Marilyn Hacker. Stillwell has published widely in a number of poetry journals, including *New York Quarterly*, *Paris Review*, *The Little Magazine*, *The Massachusetts Review*, *Confrontation*, and others, as well as in a variety of anthologies, including *Leaning into the Wind*, *The Decade Dance: A Celebration of Poems*, and *The Paris Review Anthology*. Her book of poems, *Moving to Malibu*, was published by Sandhills Press. Stillwell is coeditor of *Nebraska Presence*, an anthology of contemporary Nebraska writers published last year by Backwaters Press. Winner of a Merit Award from the Nebraska Arts Council (2006), she received her doctorate in Plains Literature from the University of Nebraska at Lincoln.

𝔈

Reunion

We are called here
to the lawn of the homestead
to look up at the face of the new red barn
and see the family brand, the IPI,
painted in white by parents.
grandparents. and their parents.
We are called to see
she has the Nollett's hair, eyes;
to see he has the Roubidoux lips, hands.
We are called to listen
to the surviving children
who sit in a circle
talking Felix, Louis, Amanda.
scarlet fever. small pox vaccinations
by their father's knife.

Later, we are called to visit
the fenced rectangle.
to hear the calls of past squaredances,
fiddles, and laughter
while our steps on the graves
move our ancestors' bones to dance.

WINTER FELL AROUND US

Winter fell around us in wide white flakes,
and we woke early,
alerted by the quiet
of the gray morning,
awoke before our fathers and grandfathers
took to the walks armed with shovels
and brooms and small thick sacks of salt,
before our mothers and grandmothers
took to the kitchen to cook snow breakfasts
of pancakes and eggs and sausage,
coffee and hot chocolate.
We sat watching the radio for signs,
listening to the smooth voices
reporting the closing of schools,
first in rural areas, small towns,
circling us, words coming closer,
until, all our senses tipped,
the day was announced ours,
and we dressed quickly.

Stiff at elbows and knees and neck from knitted things
we set out against a cold
only parents and other relatives were aware of.
The sink of the boot step,
the jump from the front steps,
and we followed the first packed tracks
up 50th Street to the corner,
circled back to the edge of the white lawn
where we paused in awe,
mounted our paints and pintos

and galloped ourselves
a corral.
And then we made small angels,
arms flapping at our sides,
and, rolling,
traced strange paths across the snow,
happy as it clung to our clothes.
Delighting in the secrets of camouflage,
we lay watching slow-moving cars.

Then up and mittens off,
we began forming the soul
round and hard,
carefully packed,
and when we held it ready in our hands
we paused again
as God might have paused at the beginning,
wondering at the possibilities of creation.
And then we fell to our knees
to roll and pack,
roll and pack again
as the body grew under our stiff hands
until it was ready
to stand by the bare branches of the lilac bush,
and we stood it there

because we remembered the lavender,
remembered the lavender against the snow.

And then we began again,
a second ball to rest upon the first,
then, quickly, the third,
our eyes rushing ahead to coal
and carrot and Grandma's apron
which, when we tied it into place,
pleased us,
and we stood back admiring
ourselves and her,
skirt flapping against imagined legs.

And sometimes passersby,
noses red and great gusts of breath on their lips,
stopped and admired, too,
before continuing their journey up Capitol Avenue.
And then our hands,
suddenly numb,
signaled lunch,
and there was a great stomping and shaking
as we entered, unwrapped ourselves,
pressed our hands against warm sides.
Steaming bowls stood waiting
beside hot toast and melted peanut butter,
and we ate with a passion
for taste, for odor,
chunks of peanut butter as welcome
as the snow had been.

And then the afternoon was imminent.
Dry socks pulled out of drawers,
mittens from radiators,
boots pulled on and buckled,
and we set out again,
this time with warnings of overdo.
Snow tracked by boots, lined with work paths.
pavement stung by salt.
we turned away to build forts
we never quite completed,
turned away from each other,
forming troops against cousins and friends,
and under the watchful eye of our snow Grandma,
and the eye of the too-soon sun.
we stockpiled snowballs.
until the first flew free from our fingers
signaling the start of battle.
our sure aim decreasing
as arms tired
and eyes tired,
and we fell silent behind our forts
and lay against the warm snow
thinking of oranges and blackboards,

hopscotch and sawhorses,
moving from one to the other
like an old jeweler
touching diamond and sapphire.
only the touch important.
Then we wanted no more of snow
and cold things.
and we rose together.

Boots heavy,
we went inside
forgetting the day
as though we had been hurt by it.
And we were sent outside again
for Grandma's apron.
and we kicked the great balls
until they fell.
and we kicked our forts to rubble.
and sometimes we kicked each other
or hit wildly until
crimson startled us from noses
as it hit like a warm heavy flake on the snow…
And sometimes there was wailing,
not because we were hurt
but because we were not hurt enough,
causing us to walk quite separately home
where it was safe.
and we could sit by ourselves
and have no thoughts at all
until supper was ready.
We ate without tasting,
looking forward to evening sounds
of television. the rattling of the evening paper.
of dishes being stacked and put away.

WALTZ

one two three
now begin
one two three
one two three
one two three
they meet un-
certainly
he steps back
she steps back
one two three
they embrace
they dance ten-
tatively
one two three
she needs his
music and
he needs her
music that
makes them dance
one two three
moving to-
gether they
dance in wide
circles they
move to the
beat that is
deep in their
wantings that
burns in their
dreamings that
touches the
beauty that
lives in their
music and
one two three
leads them to
trust in their

dancing to
love one an-
other to
move through the
night

THE THREE SISTERS

They, these gray and nameless trees,
stand, hair tossed over their heads
as though caught rinsing it.

I turn to the cherry trees,
raise their white and pink petals,
soft against the hand, but I am back
with the three sisters.
They follow me everywhere—
out of the garden,
down the street,
slide between the sheets,
grow across this page.

Oh these springs are too cold,
too short for us.
No wonder we weep so quickly,
so silently, go about bare
and barren, waiting, preparing
for the first green of summer.

SQUIRREL-HUNTING SEASON

Across the street. the trees stand nearly naked.
It's time to fold the light-weight dresses,
to pack them away, time to get out the coats and suits
and woolen things. It's squirrel-hunting season.

When I was a girl, my stepfather and I took the guns out
on Sunday afternoons. The squirrels fell heavy

from the trees and it proved something, that they
were more than leaves, our eye was quick, our aim
accurate. Then there was the skinning, I can smell
it, the smooth warm skin against the palm,
the sudden spring of the intestines against the knife,
how they glistened; this proved life and death.
Now there is rarely proof of anything,

rarely the need of it, but today, I am as nearly naked
as the trees as I fold the last dress into the trunk.
Spooks will be at the door soon enough,
and then, the snow, the need for heavy clothing.

PICKING UP THE BALES

There are four of us now
to pick up the bales,
to balance them for the sharp turns
that lead to the barn.

I drive the Massey that pulls
the wagon, and because it is new to me,
my mother rides the fender,
shot gun, she says, watches for washings

along the terraces. My brother lifts
the bales to the hay rack; my stepfather
stacks. Alfalfa flies as green and as quick
as grasshoppers around them.

It comes back gradually, and by afternoon,
I go easily between the rows, judge weight
by the curve of my brother's spine. Bales
are light here; we move quickly. Bales
grow heavy here and I slow.

BARTON SUTTER ℘

Barton Sutter was raised in small towns in the Upper Midwest and graduated from Southwest Minnesota State University in 1972 with a B.A. in language arts. He earned an M.A. in creative writing from Syracuse University in 1975. For ten years, Sutter worked as a printer (Boston and Minneapolis) and then made his living as a freelance writer and part-time instructor at various institutions, including St. John's University; the University of Minnesota - Twin Cities; and the University of Minnesota - Duluth. He has published poems, essays, and stories in dozens of magazines and produced six books. *My Father's War and Other Stories* (Viking, 1991, University of Minnesota 2000) won the 1992 Minnesota Book Award in Fiction. *The Book of Names: New and Selected Poems* (BOA Editions, 1993) won the 1994 Minnesota Book Award for Poetry. For several years, Sutter wrote and broadcast monthly commentaries for Minnesota Public Radio, and these essays were collected in *Cold Comfort: Life at the Top of the Map* (Univeristy of Minnesota, 1998), which won both the 1999 Minnesota Book Award for Creative Non-fiction and the Northeastern Minnesota Book Award. In 2005, Sutter won the George Morrison Artist Award for his contribution to the arts in northeastern Minnesota. In 2006, he was named the first Poet Laureate of Duluth. He has received other awards from the Academy of American Poets, The Jerome Foundation, The Loft, and the Arrowhead Regional Arts Council. The poems included here are from *Pine Creek Parish Hall and Other Poems* (1985).

℘

GENEVA

She was famous for kindness, Geneva.
And yet she could run down a hen
And chop off its head just like that.
"Macaroni!" I said, when I saw the insides,
And she crowed like a satisfied rooster.
I once watched her husband, the only man
I knew who had a mustache, string up
And slaughter a cow. I ran to Geneva
And buried my face in her lap. "Geneva,"
I said, "does it hurt?" "That old cow?"
Said Geneva. "Don't worry," she said.
"You don't feel a thing when you're dead."

Geneva giggled and taught me to piss
In the dark in a thunder jug.
I was from town and embarrassed,
But Geneva enjoyed that noise.
She taught me itchweed and outhouse.
She spanked me and wiped my ass.
She was a good one, Geneva.
The world was a joke, and everyone said:
"She's a real card, that Geneva."

She had warts and a nose, Geneva,
And a twisted smile with teeth,
But she also had beautiful daughters.
Hay and fresh faces and breasts.
They could cook. The kitchen had pails,
And everyone drank from the dipper.
I can taste the tang of the tin
And smell that slop-bucket stink
And the fragrance of bread on the table.
She was always baking, Geneva.

She taught me the stars, Geneva.
It was night. In the garden.
She was giving us something again:

Carrots, cucumbers, tomatoes, and such,
Everything cool and slick. "Chicken shit,'
Said Geneva. "That's the secret," she said.
My pants were all wet with the dew.
"Look at that," said Geneva

And showed me the star-spangled sky.
"It's a coloring book," said Geneva.
"It's all dot-to-dot. Don't you see?"
And I saw: The Sisters, The Hunter,
The Bull and The Bear, The Dipper
From which we all drank.

So I thank the stars for Geneva,
All of her muscles and fat, that
Quick chicken-killer, that ugly
She of the beautiful daughters
And prize-winning hogs, that woman
Of pickles and jam. Geneva,
She taught me the mud and the stars,
And when I am ready to die
She will come with her hatchet in hand
And her face like a kerosene lamp
And her dress all feathers and blood.

Halloween on Hennepin

It's Halloween going on midnight. Boo.
So what's happening? The usual Hennepin Avenue
Sideshow, only more so: a parade
Of pimps in costumes custom-made
With sequins, studs, and stars enough
To knock your eye out; renegade Sioux;
A few blue policemen; a dwarf
Or two for good measure;
Roughnecks on every corner;
A regular cakewalk of whores.
What you see is what you get
For naming streets after Jesuits.

Poor old Father Hennepin.
He thought the Indians were pagan.
If he knew how his namesake needs him,
He'd come back to haunt the heathen.
And maybe he's here, for Christ's sake.
A queer, forgiving attitude
Mingles with the fumes on the avenue
Tonight. The usual goofballs don't seem sick.
This fag in drag, for instance, skirt slit
Up to the crotch, silk shirt
Pregnant with foam rubber knockers.
Hobbled by heels that have to hurt,
He can hardly walk. He does an imitation,
A drunken, awkward, hippety hopscotch
That draws applause from streetwalkers.
Still, the mockery has limitations.
If you want to be your sister,
It's okay, Mister. We'd rather
Be someone else, ourselves. And those of us
Coming off nightshift, going on graveyard,
Plainclothes people, waiting for the bus,
Take a different attitude
Toward the prostitutes tonight.
What the hell? We're all co-workers.
When a hooker with a puss
Like a jack-o-lantern offers,
"Hello, Luv." I answer,
And we chat about the weather
And the costumes until she pushes off.
People returning from parties pass
For Frankenstein and Dracula,
A horse's head and a horse's ass,
A pretty pair of nuns.
The guy beside me asks,
"What's black and white
And black and white and black and white?"
"A nun falling down stairs," I laugh.
"Everyone knows that one."
Finally our coach arrives,
And the stumblebums with shopping bags,

Hungry bachelors, working wives,
All board. Soon the doors flap open
For the hobbledehoy with plastic legs
And aluminum sticks, who lugs
Himself around by hand
Like a broken-backed amphibian.
The biddy ahead of me meows,
"Poor soul," as always,
And looks away out the window.
A nurse gets up to leave and sways
Like laundry on the line. The burgundy blot
She wears across her heart
Is not a carnation. Tomorrow
I'll be more than half afraid
Of this grim carnival,
This motley masquerade.
All this fellow feeling will sour
Into lonesome fury, sure
As I'll be sitting here. Now, though,
I'm confused by affection.
Spooky. Almost Christian.
Not knowing exactly what I mean,
I say to the stranger beside me,
"Hey. Happy Halloween."

SHOE SHOP

I shut the door on the racket
Of rush hour traffic,
Inhale the earthy, thick
Perfume of leather and pipe tobacco.

The place might be a barbershop
Where the air gets lathered with gossip.
You can almost hear the whippersnap
Of the straightedge on the razor strop.

It might be a front for agitators,
But there's no back room. A rabble

Of boots and shoes lies tumbled
In heaps like a hoard of potatoes.

The cobbler, broad as a blacksmith,
Turns a shoe over his pommel,
Pummels the sole, takes the nail
He's bit between his teeth

And drives it into the heel. Hunched
At his workbench, he pays the old shoe
More attention than me. "Help you?"
He grunts, as if the man held a grudge

Against business. He gives my run-over
Loafer a look. "Plastic," he spits.
"And foreign-made. Doubt I can fix it."
I could be holding a dead gopher.

"The Europeans might make good shoes,
But I never see them. Cut the price.
Advertise! Never mind the merchandise.
You buy yourself a pair, brand new,

"The welt will be cardboard
Where it ought to be leather.
There's nothing to hold the shoe together."
He stows my pair in a cupboard.

"And all of them tan with acid.
The Mexicans make fancy boots, but they cure
Their leather in cow manure. Wear
Them out in the rain once. Rancid?

"I had a guy bring me a pair.
Wanted me to get rid of the stink.
Honest to God. I hate to think
My customers are crazy, but I swear."

He curses factories, inflation,
And I welcome the glow of conspiracy.

Together we plot, half seriously,
A counter industrial revolution.

His pride's been steeped in bitterness,
His politics tanned with elbow-grease.
To hear him fume and bitch, you'd guess
His guerrilla warfare's hopeless.

But talk about job satisfaction!
To take a tack from a tight-lipped smile,
Stick it like a thorn in an unworn sole,
To heft the hammer, and whack it!

When I step back out in the street
The city looks flimsy as a movie set.

SWEDISH LESSON

Talk about the mother tongue.
I heard these words when I was young.
I'd gabble gibberish and stutter,
Mimicking my babysitters.
They'd say, "Can you speak svenska?"
I'd answer, "Ya, you betcha."
They'd giggle, slap their laps, and sigh.
Their gossip was my lullabye.
Around the barn their men would grunt
The Esperanto of immigrants.

My grandmother risked ridicule
Whenever she opened her mouth at school
But broke the brogue. I speak American,
But, feeling like a bad translation,
I bought the books and paid tuition.
My classmates mock my pronunciation.

Once these words were hawked and spit
By barbarians who meant it
When they swore. They drew swords

225

And mangled men for what they said.
These words are theirs but tamed by time,
Their history a wind chime.
Hearsay now, they sound so gentle
I think of women spinning wool.
Chuckling like a dandling song,
The melodic nonsense passes on
Rumors of the old country. We
Hear the schuss of snow and ski
Past places parents mentioned.
Strange. The teacher's intonation
Makes every other word a question.

Blue-collar misfits, dissatisfied
Housewives, we've stood beside
Our ancestors, laid hands on headstones,
Wondering why they ever left home,
Mystified by the rotten spoils
Of the Viking dream of silk and jewels.
We've traced the foreign, familiar names
Chiseled in grim cuneiform.
The rune stones resist interpretation.

And so we've begun this reverse migration.
God knows what we hope to learn.
The motives of the arctic tern?
We murmur, uncertain what we're about,
But, counting together, we launch the boat.
I swear by my grandmother's face
And steer to the north, northeast.
I stammer and repeat my faith
In the dead, their hope, their anguish,
Buried alive in this, their language.

ANN TOWNSEND ℰℒ

Ann Townsend is the author of two collections of poetry: *The Coronary Garden* (2005) and *Dime Store Erotics* (1998), and editor (with David Baker) of *Radiant Lyre: Essays on Lyric Poetry* (2008). Her poems have appeared in such magazines as *Poetry*, *The Paris Review*, *The Nation*, *Witness*, *The Georgia Review*, and many others. She is the recipient of a National Endowment for the Arts Fellowship, an Individual Artist's grant from the Ohio Arts Council, and a Discovery Prize from *The Nation*. Her poems have appeared in many anthologies, including *The Pushcart Prize XX*, *The New Young American Poets*, *American Poetry: The Next Generation*, and *The New American Poets: A Bread Loaf Anthology*. Dominic Consolo Professor of English and Director of Creative Writing at Denison University, she lives on a small farm in Granville, Ohio.

The poems collected here are from *Holding Katherine*, a Main-Travelled Roads chapbook.

ℰℒ

FIRST LANGUAGE

You say *hi* to the soft face
of the TV mommy who sings and scrubs a kitchen
while her boys track mud again across the floor.
This spring black ants soldier in busy pairs
beneath the door frames, harbingers of rain,
and you've lifted one to your lips
before I call see what's wrong
as you cry *hi, hi, hi*
and paw your tongue with helpless hands,
I see the ant stapled
hard to your tongue. He won't come loose,
I doctor you with cups of water;

You gag, wail, laugh. It's fun to cough.
Nearly, you forget the ant.
He doesn't forget you. Only with tweezers
does he detach, piece by piece
from your tongue, until at last the dark head
and sharp pincers are left behind,
sour dot, raisin you cannot eat,
here at the center of our insufficiency,
the new syllables breaking from your mouth.

IN A MOMENT

She drives alone and quickly
on a snow-blasted highway
no cars, only the salt kiss
of the semis as they steam by.

Jazz on the radio, in and out
with the storm's static fuzz,
and through the night haze
the searchlights of the auto mall

scrape the sky in wild arcs.
In the hospital where she left
her daughter finally sleeping
in her crib, nurses whisper

behind a high desk and hurry
to monitors buzzing, the sound of emergency.
There are women walking two floors below,
holding big bellies before them,

counting down the heartbeats,
inscribing their pain
in the half-moon fingernail marks
they leave on their lovers' forearms.

The child turns,

restless in her room, to the crib's
high slats and the oxygen machine
purring. She has opened her eyes

in a perpetual half-light
to watch the unfamiliar mobile spin overhead,
its pastels bleached grey by the night.

Now cars rush past the lonely exit ramp
where, snow frosted, engine humming,
one idles off the road,
and a woman inside lets the world
fill up with snow.

SORROW

It's in the air between us
as the next true moment
after I yell, tear sheets away,
spring from bed and you, faster,
grapple, wrestle me back
from the bedroom door.
Our hands slap at each other
as our *sorry, sorry* strikes the air.

The baby's furious wails
have penetrated even the earplugs
you wear to seal yourself
off at night, so you know
I hurry not to calm her, but to kill.
She's choked on a cough
so deep it blankets her lungs;
I'm shoving your hands away,

until at last we touch our own
nature, to go to her
with the false semblance of calm,
together, to boost her

to the window ledge
where the fat moon waits
like a white face
that cries from the deep black sky.

WILLIAM TROWBRIDGE ☙

William Trowbridge's poetry publications include *The Complete Book of Kong* (Southeast Missouri State University Press, 2003), *Flickers*, *O Paradise*, and *Enter Dark Stranger* (University of Arkansas Press, 2000, 1995, 1989), and three chapbooks, *The Packinghouse Cantata* (Camber Press, 2006), *The Four Seasons* (Red Dragonfly Press, 2001) and *The Book of Kong* (Iowa State University Press, 1986). His poems have appeared in more than 30 anthologies and textbooks, as well as in such periodicals as *Poetry*, *The Gettysburg Review*, *Crazyhorse*, *The Georgia Review*, *Boulevard*, *The Southern Review*, *Columbia*, *Colorado Review*, *The Iowa Review*, *Prairie Schooner*, *Epoch*, and *New Letters*. He has given readings and workshops at schools, colleges, bookstores, and literary conferences throughout the United States. His awards include an Academy of American Poets Prize, a Bread Loaf Writers' Conference scholarship, and fellowships from The MacDowell Colony, Ragdale, Yaddo, and The Anderson Center. He is Distinguished University Professor Emeritus at Northwest Missouri State University and was an editor of *The Laurel Review* from 1986 to 2004. The poems here were included in *Decade Dance*.

☙

ENTER DARK STRANGER

In *Shane*, when Jack Palance first appears,
a stray cur takes one look and slinks away
on tiptoes, able, we understand, to recognize
something truly dark. So it seems
when we appear, crunching through the woods.
A robin cocks her head, then hops off,
ready to fly like hell and leave us the worm.
A chipmunk, peering out from his hole
beneath a maple root, crash dives
when he hears our step. The alarm spreads in a skittering
of squirrels, finches, millipedes. Imagine

a snail picking up the hems of his shell
and hauling ass for cover. He's studied carnivores,
seen the menu, noticed the escargots.

But forget Palance, who would have murdered Alabama
just for fun. Think of Karloff's monster,
full of lonely love but too hideous
to bear; or Kong, bereft with Fay Wray
shrieking in his hand: the flies circle our heads
like angry biplanes, and the ants hoist pitchforks
to march on our ankles as we watch the burgher's daughter
bob downstream in a ring of daisies.

SCORCHER

July, and our team's burned up
again. We watch them sweat on TV
when the cable's working. At twelve
games out, the rookie pitcher changed
his number and finally won one,
then broke his wrist. He wants to be
traded. The owner says he'll have to wait
in line. Today it got so hot
a pigeon stuck in the asphalt
outside Nora's Hair Clinique and just
stood there--waiting for cars,
maybe, hoping to get it quick
and head on. Drivers, even ones
whose air conditioners still work,
are too hot to notice birds
or children. We're running short
of water, electricity, our famous
Midwestern patience and plain-
spoken ways. Sarcasm's spread
like Asian flu. People ask you where
you learned to drive or how you got
your head so far up your ass. Gun racks
in pickups fill as if it's
deer season. Some new season

may be near. Our tornado in 1962
and our lynching in 1932 are recalled
these days with something past nostalgia
as the grass curls into browner straw
and the Johnson weed encroaches
on our suburb, where the bank
president and the doctor, both away
in Palm Springs till September,
live. The forecast for tomorrow
is 105 with a thick blue fog
of pollen and mold spores. We feel
like colonists on Mars. No one can tell us
how we wound up in a place like this.
Meanwhile our team, who's never heard
of us, sits out the All-Star Game,
which is on tonight, preempting "Dynasty."
Maybe we'll watch it anyway, maybe not.

WALKING BACK

I have no business here, a bearded stranger
circling the block, beginning to draw looks
from the man pruning his forsythia, the housewife
who calls the children in from jump rope.
Dutch elm disease has thinned the landscape,
let afternoon sunlight glare off grass and sidewalks.
Everything looks too new. Our house is green now,
with patio and lawn where tufts of rye grass
used to stall our mower till my father
took to working weekends at the office.
Even our front-yard maple's forgotten
my mark beneath thirty-five new rings.
Up the street, Skrija's grocery store
has lost its musty heart of oak
and penny candy. A neon sign announces
"Guns and Ammo" above barred windows
and a yellow metal door. Still, there's the
bump at Sixtieth and Grove--ready as ever
for the next no-hander showing off for his idea

of the girl who'd like his looks--and the blue jays
and the locusts and the tack of ripe asphalt.

Like those who stare, I wonder what I want,
whether I'm dangerous or simply need directions.
Today, hundreds, maybe thousands of us search
the old neighborhoods for clues: initials in a sidewalk,
a rusty nail pounded in a tree, a wish still floating
near the school, where a small ghost, waiting
on the last bell, rubs the shiny nickel in his pocket.

Ronald Wallace ❧

Ronald Wallace is the author of numerous poetry collections, including *For a Limited Time Only* (2008), *Long for This World: New & Selected Poems* (2003), and the Wisconsin Library Association Banta Award–winner *Time's Fancy* (1994), as well as the linked story collection *Quick Bright Things: Stories* (2000). His critical writing includes *God Be With the Clown: Humor in American Poetry* (1984), *The Last Laugh: Form and Affirmation in the Contemporary American Comic Novel* (1979), and *Henry James and the Comic Form* (1975). Wallace also edited the anthology *Vital Signs: Contemporary American Poetry* from the University Presses (1989).

Wallace is the founder and co-director of the Program in Creative Writing at the University of Wisconsin-Madison, where he is Felix Pollak Professor of Poetry and Halls-Bascom Professor of English. He lives on a 40-acre farm in Richland County, Wisconsin.

The work collected here comes from *Worry*, a Main-Travelled Roads chapbook.

Note from Wallace About Sandhills Press: No Worries

I can worry about anything, from the serious to the trivial, from the momentous to the mundane. It is an integral part of my personality, and, consequently, of my poetry and fiction. Every book I have published over the past thirty years has included at least one piece (often more) specifically devoted to the subject of worry.

Thus, in 1996 when Mark Sanders invited me to provide a manuscript for the second chapbook in his innovative Main-Traveled Roads series (a central purpose of which was to make new work, particularly work in genres or modes or directions which a given writer may not previously have attempted, available, with as little lag time as possible between submission and publication), I was delighted to send him my first foray into fiction, a chapbook of short-short stories entitled (what else?)

Worry. Of course, I worried that he wouldn't like it, and that I should probably stick to poetry, and would never write fiction again.

But like it he did, and, with speed and affection, published a lovely little chapbook complete with his own cover drawing that perfectly captured the spirit of the title story. But it was more than a lovely little chapbook; it was a confidence builder that reinforced my desire to write more and longer fiction and led to the completion of my novel-in-stories, *Quick Bright Things*, published by Midlist Press in 2000.

The chapbook series, like everything else Mark has done over the years (founding and editing Sandhills Press, producing *On Common Ground, The Plains Poetry Series, The Sandhills & Other Geographies, The Sandhills II, The Decade Dance*, the magazine *Hurakan*, all of which expanded the audience for both regional and nationally acclaimed writers) was a wonderful success, and I am grateful to have been included in it.

There are a lot of things to worry about on the literary scene these days, and, God knows, I'm worrying. But Mark Sanders and his continuing projects aren't among them. Nope. No worries there!

℘

HAY

"That's a nice barn you got there, Adams," Heller says, rocking back on his heels, pausing to make some small adjustment in the crotch of his bib overalls. "A guy could put some hay in that barn. You got any hay?"

He already has his heifers in our meadow, his machines in our shed, and his chickens in our chicken house. We had originally bought the forty acre property – an abandoned house and buildings, a steep brushy hillside, a small meadow – as a weekend and summer retreat. "An investment," my wife said. "An expensive toy," I said. Now we live here permanently, my wife restoring prairie and gardening, while I commute the eighty miles daily to Fidelity Mutual Life and Casualty in Milwaukee.

The first day we spent on the property, assessing the caved-in porch roof, the rotting king beam in the basement, the broken pump ("A dream," my wife said; "A nightmare," I said), Heller appeared. He had wanted to buy the place himself. He couldn't believe anyone would pay what old man Iams was asking. He loomed over me like a doomed outbuilding. "You gonna put any machines in that shed?"

He never asked outright for anything. He didn't *need* any other buildings, he had plenty of buildings, he said. Still, I wouldn't mind, would I, if he put some wood in the woodshed, some corn in the corn crib, some grain in the granary.

My wife seemed to like him. "A real operator," she said, with some inexplicable admiration in her eyes.

"Nope, no hay," I say, knowing the barn will be full tomorrow.

Heller smiles, his gold front tooth gleaming as he gazes across the large front yard to Evelyn working hard in the garden. He puts his hands in his pockets and rocks back comfortably. "That's a good-lookin' woman you got there," he says.

WRESTLING

"Have you thought about your college wardrobe yet?" she says.

"My *what?*" I reply, pinning her arm behind her back.

"Your wardrobe," she says. She grabs my hair and pulls hard, "When I went to college, I remember how I coordinated my skirts and blouses and shoes. My shoes were gray and brown and blue and pink so they would go with anything."

I have her in a half-nelson now. "Don't worry about me," I say.

She slams me into the corner cupboard and kicks her heel into my shin. "And what about this vegetarian diet of yours? How will you get enough protein?"

As the pain shoots through my kneecap I pull her to the ground. I could comment on her peacock blue polyester pants suit, or the cows she murders for meat, but I don't. I get her in a hammerlock. "I guess I'm going to miss you," I say, with only the slightest tinge of irony.

I've almost got her pinned, but she manages to wrench over onto her stomach. "You probably won't be attending church much, either, I suppose."

Somehow she's managed to flip me and I'm straining under her weight. "Just let go, why don't you?" I grimace.

She gets me in a scissors grip, and squeezes. "I know, you're on your own now, dear. I know."

I'm breathing hard, confused by her sudden maneuver. I can see God's hand hovering above the mat as my shoulders arch and twist. The crowd hoots and whistles. I'm down, but I'm not out. In my corner, the future is waving, shouting its loud instructions. I know what I have to do.

"I love you," I tell her. "I love you."

And she's down for the count.

WORRY

She worried about people: he worried about things. And between them, that about covered it.

"What would you think of our daughter sleeping around?" she said.

"The porch steps are rotting," he replied. "Someone's going to fall through."

They were lying in bed together, talking. They had been lying in bed together talking these twenty-five years: first, about whether to have children – he wanted to (although the roof was going fast); she didn't (Down's Syndrome. Leukemia, microcephalia, mumps) – and then, after their daughter was born – a healthy seven pounds eleven ounces ("She's not eating enough"; "The furnace is failing") – about family matters mostly ("Her friends are hoodlums, her room is a disaster"; "There's something about the brakes, the water heater's rusting out").

Worry grew between them like a son, with his own small insistencies and then more pressing demands. They stroked and coddled him; they set a place for him at the table; they sent him to kindergarten, private school, and college. Because he failed at nearly everything and always returned home, they loved him. After all, he was their son.

"I've been reading her diary. She does drugs. She sleeps around."

"I just don't think I can fix them myself. Where will we find a carpenter?"

And so it went. Their daughter married her high school sweetheart, had a family, and started a health food store in a distant town. Although she recalled her childhood as fondly as anyone – how good her parents had been and how they worried for her, how old and infirm they must be growing. their house going to ruin – she rarely called or visited. She had worries of her own.

DON WELCH &

Poet Don Welch is a Nebraska native and the author of many collections of poetry, including *Dead Horse Table*, *Handwork*, *The Rarer Game*, *The Keeper of Miniature Deer*, *The Marginalist*, *Every Mouth of Autumn Says Goodbye*, *The Breeder of Archangels / Requiem for Stanley Smith*, *Inklings: Poems Old and New*, and *The Alley Poems*. His most recent book is *Gnomes* (SFA Press, 2013). In 1980 he won the Pablo Neruda Prize for Poetry, judged by William Stafford. He holds a BA from Kearney State, an MA from the University of Northern Colorado, and a PhD from the University of Nebraska - Lincoln. He retired as Reynolds Professor of Literature at the University of Nebraska - Kearney. He lives in Kearney with his wife, Marcia, and is a long-time racer of homing pigeons.

NOTE FROM WELCH ABOUT SANDHILLS PRESS

A tip of my cup to the Sandhills Press for celebrating the uncommon ground upon which poets make their stands; for three decades of dancing the best poems into our eyes; and for pinching from pennies some very remarkable books.

*

For decades now two people have been leaving an imprint upon Nebraska, zillionaire Ted Turner with his ranches, and poem-steader Mark Sanders of the Sandhills Press.

As a squatter myself, I'll drink to the latter.

*

The Sandhills Press is to poetry what the Nebraska Sandhills are to the endangered plant, the blow-out penstemon, an eco-system which keeps a rare species alive.

*

In that semi-arid region called the Nebraska Sandhills grows the yucca, with its rosettes of evergreen leaves and panicles of white flowers. What better emblem for a tough-rooted and attractive poetry press.

*

You would think from its title The Sandhills Press would be narrow and provincial, but like the short-, mixed-, and tall grass prairie which comprises the grass hills of Nebraska, it continues to surprise us with its subtleties of tastes.

*

No one knows how tough it is to keep a small press going. Right now, where you are, is a good time to guess.

*

Here's to the Sandhills Press. May it always draw upon an aquifer of interest. And in the face of it, keep turning in the wind.

ℰꙅ

CARVED BY OBADIAH VERITY

Once when I was looking at some decoys
carved a hundred years ago,
curlews and plovers, ruddy tumstones,
I thought of how they began,
as stutters in wood, gouges and flutes,
skewers and judgments of beauty.

They were simple things.

In their heartwoods the grains ran on,
the primitive music of fibers.
And as I stood there I began to imagine
Verity working, the acts of his hands,
the pauses, in which he kept

mounting something finer than skin
on those things. And what came over
the years was more than a touchable
silence. There was something
in those shore birds I was supposed
to pass on, from Verity,

like the deep intelligence of love,
and I left that place full of
breed and brood and cross-hatching.

FUNERAL AT ANSLEY

I write of a cemetery,
of the perpetual care of buffalo grass,
of kingbirds and catbirds
and cottonwoods;

of wild roses around headstones,
with their high thin stems
and their tight tines
and their blooms pursed
in the morning.

I write of old faces,
of cotton hose and flowered dresses
and mouths which have grown up
on the weather.

And I write of one woman
who lies a last time in the long sun
of August, uncramped by the wind
which autumns each one of us

under catbirds and kingbirds
and cottonwoods, and the gray-green
leaves of the buffalo grass.

THE KEEPER OF MINIATURE DEER

The keeper of miniature deer
was an old man with stiff knees.
He had the straight eyes of a child,
and he walked the emperor's grounds
speaking to the white swans
and the empress's pheasants.
In the compound of red deer,
among the musk and estrus,
he was especially fond of two old ones
born joined at the shoulders,
a stag with its rack huge and carbuncular
spreading out over a doe,
the old doe with eyes like fitful oil
over water. And he who knew nothing
of life after death, who lived
only to serve the miniature deer,
let them eat from his hands,
holding out salt in one,
in the other, grain,
softly calling their names,
saying, *Mother* and *Father.*

NEBRASKA

Going west when the sun is going down,
following the highways like light cords.

*

If Nebraska were the name of a Russian woman,
they could love her.

There would be a certain large-boned beauty about her.

Or she would be dressed in black and lace.
Her waist would be small,
and she would drag her long dress over a floor
into a study lined with French books.

She would be a pawn in huge novels of war.

*

As it is, she is a woman of spare beauty.

*

Turning away from him so that the fine hollows
of her back were toward the bed,
she said, Why do you do this to me?

Why do you keep imagining me in other places
and states?

And why do you keep assuming our children
are unhappy?

NEVER WRITE IN A GLASS HOUSE

Never write in a glass house,
the least spirit dies for the want of matter
In winter, barely vertebrate,
souls shiver in dry grass.

Like wheat stubble, they're reduced
to playing children of the lowest god,
and common's their tongue
which wants to raise itself to lilt.

Last summer, morning glories

kept asking where the sun was headed,
their fragile loves blue witnesses
to August's moments.

As we age, summer is the first to go,
then spring. What's youth
if not our bodies making light
of our spirits' shades?

THE RARER GAME

1. The Mute Swans

A sign on the park fence told us what they were:
MUTE SWANS, ORIGIN ENGLAND,
WEIGHT EXCEEDING FIFTEEN POUNDS.

They swam alone, unreeling our attention.

With their rinds of feathers, meat of white,
the graceful extensions of their necks.

How much of the world they had to shed
in just pushing themselves along.

How beneath the whiteness of their forms
such black legs churned.

Our children were trying to trick the geese
into eating ice cubes.

The swans swam on,
serious, complete, of such a certain magnitude.

But their flaw was not their muteness;
each wild length ended
in a clipped wing.

How at night

they had to put themselves to sleep
behind that one clipped thing.

2. The Snow Geese

After the first snow
an edge comes on.
The dew that has gathered itself
all fall on the roof,
loosing itself from the eaves,
now stays, hard in the sun.
The roof is a sum
of its brilliant selves,
a white explosion of nerves.

North of the house
snow geese stand in a field,
silent, their acts pulled down,
their orange bills in the cold
announcing themselves.

Suddenly I'm up
putting my hands on the pane,
wanting out with those geese.
My hands and wrists and arms
are fuses abroad with the cold.

And when the geese turn,
short bodies, their shadows firm
against the ground, I want to go forth
over and over again in the snow,
putting my flat hands down.

3. The Bull Elk

Even after he walked up to it,
crumpled on the ground,
there was a wrenched silence
to the place.

He bled the head downhill.
He cut along the belly line
from the brisket to the vent.
He went deeper through the muscles.

Pulling up, he used his fingers
as guides, slabbing himself
through the stiffening intentions
of its legs.

He avoided the intestines,
he went around the anus,
he split the pelvic bones.
Straddling back toward the head,

he used an axe to split
the chest, front to back,
then followed the gullet
and windpipe to the tongue.

Cutting both, he pulled.
The heart, liver, lungs,
and paunch came out.
The rumen he threw away,

what was left of the Trembling
Aspen and the Rose. He stepped
back from straddling the head,
he wiped his hands.

The tongue was simply thicker
than it had ever been.

4. The Eider

Far out in this ocean of a river
the eider ducks, drifting in rafts, in sanctuaries,
are huge birds, stark white above
and black below.

Moniacs, the Eskimos call them,
saying they line their nest with down,
working their bills as far
into their breasts as nature allows.

Not eating when they brood.

They say that when they come back from drinking
there is a long low croon of birds over the water,
in the dusk a line of beads
workings its way back to the nest.

And then the brooding begins again,
and then the dark comes down.

5. The Hawk

Somewhere years from now
I hope I'm saying this
to my sons. Why the hawk
had hit the trap I couldn't guess.
In the face of it
it was pointless.

But it had hit the trigger
dead center with both feet,
for a moment lifting
that fatal weight
before the blind torque
of the trap had sprung.

After that its wings had clawed
at the sand for hours,
its cries had gradually sunk back
into its throat, although
its beak, thrust defiantly
at the stream, held on
to its animal yellow.

Then it had pulled everything in,
for a moment the hawk
and only the hawk's turn;
in that blind and beautiful light,
trying to hold on,
as the trap held on,
to what it was.

KATHLEENE WEST &

Kathleene West grew up on a farm three miles west of Genoa, Nebraska. She was educated at the University of Washington and the University of Nebraska - Lincoln, where she earned her PhD in English Literature. She published several books of poetry and fiction, her most recent being the novel *The Summer of the Sub-comandante*. Other books include *Death of a Regional Poet, Canto 1* (Main-Travelled Roads #13, 1998), *Water Witching* (Copper Canyon, 1984), *The Farmer's Daughter* (Sandhills, 1990), *Plainswoman: Her First Hundred Years* (Sandhills, 1985), *The Garden Section* (Yellow Barn Press, 1982), *Land Bound* (Copper Canyon Press, 1978), and *The Armadillo on the Rug* (Seal Press, 1978). She was awarded a Fulbright Fellowship to Iceland for two years, a National Endowment of the Arts apprenticeship award, and Honorable Mention in the Binational Border Poetry Contest (Mexico and the United States). During her lifetime, she had lectured and given readings of her poems in the United States, Iceland, China, Mexico, Cuba, and the Dominican Republic. Following her retirement from New Mexico State University, she committed suicide in 2013, although preparations from her last book of poetry were well underway. This posthumous collection, *Tourists of the Revolution*, was published in 2014.

NOTE FROM WEST ABOUT SANDHILLS PRESS:
From Diplomatic Sleight-of-Hand to a Byronic Saga
30 Years With Sandhills Press

In Fall 1984 when I was living in Iceland on a Fulbright fellowship, I received word of a manuscript competition for a new Nebraska press, Sandhills Press, edited by Jim Brummels and Mark Sanders. I had a manuscript nearly completed, the first part of a projected trilogy, with the working title of "Plainswoman," and I hoped to have the first book to be published in Nebraska. The deadline for the manuscript was fast approaching, but while I was fussing with section titles and last-minute revisions, a series of strikes swept Iceland. That, for the next six weeks, meant no newspapers, no news programs on radio or television, no incoming or outgoing flights, no mail, and none of the imported goods the isolated island depended on. One of my professors at Háskóli Íslands

(The University of Iceland) said "It's just like the war (WW II)." Only the once-a-week diplomatic flights and military flights from the Keflavík American base continued, neither of which had any connection with we who lived there.

In my journal dated October 11, 1985 I wrote: "Plainswoman: Her First Hundred Years" is ready for flójtrit (air mail), ready to pop in an envelope and pray for the strike to be over or to plead with Ken Yates through Robert to let it go off in embassy 'official business' mail.'" Robert Berman, the Fulbright Director in Iceland, was doubtful; but he agreed to try to convince Yates, the new Chair of the Fulbright Commission in Iceland as well as a diplomat at the American Embassy, to include my manuscript with official business and "smuggle" (my word) it out of Iceland. Yates was proud of his re-organization of the Icelandic Fulbright Commission, and I think was suspicious of any request that didn't fit in his idea of specifications and guidelines; but eventually he agreed to include my manuscript with the embassy mail.

The diplomatic flight was to Copenhagen, Denmark; I had to depend on some anonymous staffer to mail it from there to the United States. I had no way of knowing if the manuscript would get to the US, much less Nebraska, in time.

Journal entry, Iceland, February 2, 1985: "Plainswoman, Part I" is accepted. Barbara (my sister) calls to tell me." Three days later I received the official acceptance letter from Jim Brummels.

Journal entry, Lincoln, Nebraska, September 21, 1985: "The Plainswoman proofs are here from Mark Sanders—in Palatino (font) and looking good." *Plainswoman* sold out relatively quickly; it appeared on a number of reading lists of university and college courses, especially in Nebraska.

My other publications with Sandhills were under less dramatic circumstances, but I've never ceased to be thrilled by the publication of a new book. *The Farmer's Daughter* came out while I was professor at New Mexico State University, as did the chapbook, *Death of a Regional Poet, Canto One*, number 13 of Mark's Main-Traveled Roads chapbook series.

Although it seems that Sandhills Press is most often associated with printing and encouraging poems from a certain region, for me, Mark Sanders is also an editor who is willing to take chances. The manuscript "Death of a Regional Poet" is a mock-epic, influenced by Bryon's *Don Juan*, right down to the ottava rima stanza he used, along with a healthy dose of his sarcasm and satire, making it appear to most editors as an anachronism. The book was truly *ars gratia artis*, a book I'd written in one of those Romantic-poets trances in less than three months. I felt the book was a suitable response to one of *Plainswoman's* critics who felt that the heroine of PW was "too noble"; there was little sentimentalism in "Death of a Regional Poet." I really wanted at least part of the manuscript published while my then-ninety-year-old father lived, and Mark was willing to publish the first Canto in his Main-Traveled Roads chapbook series as *Death of a Regional Poet, Canto One.*

Sandhills Press has been part of my publishing and writing career throughout its existence. I am pleased to help celebrate its anniversary.

❧

THE GARDEN PLOT

I will please the spirits of this place.

I will dig my fingers into the earth.

I will feel the dirt rim my fingertips
as it begins the total eclipse of my skin.

As my mother and her mother before
buried a spoon beneath the house
to charm the malevolent troll
I force my fingers deep
and the seeds descend
little saviours that wait for rain
to burst their sepulchres
and transfigure the plain.

We are here to grow.

I am on my knees
sprinkling the soil over the blank rows
crossing my palms on their promise.

Below

the spirits gather
rude and demanding as children
caressing, pressing the turnips
clinging to rhubarb's fingers
pink and pale.

I have gifts.

I fill the earth
with the garden's sweet offer
potato sprouts, frail tomatoes
the gentle bite of radish
and beetroot, its thickness, its flesh.

I whisper to the spirits.

It is not enough to survive.

The crisp aisles of lettuce
lead me down
to the candelabra of squash
the suppliant
succulent bean.

I bend low over the earth
and nurture as I praise
praise this vegetable paradise.

Ethereal carrot tops!

Ascending onion!

I bid you grow
grow and be beautiful.

GRANDMOTHER'S GARDEN

As she loved harvest when the final ear hit the bangboard
as she loved the exquisite snip and tie of huck embroidery
as she loved her children quiet in Sunday best
as she loved all beauty and the reward of rest after work
        she loved her flowers.

And when he took a hacksaw
and cut wide swaths, like a scythe through grain,
slicing high the stems of tulip and iris
to make impossible even a salvaged bouquet,
she turned back to the house
and busied herself with some kitchen task
to wait for the child, who ran from the shattered blooms,
her small fists clenched on a few ripped petals,
her breath lost in the flattened bed of bouncing betts.

"Grandma, he's killing your flowers!"

And Grandmother winked,
        yes,
        winked

as if to say:

I'm not angry
but don't let on to Grandpa.
If he saw I didn't mind
it'd hurt him more
than whatever hurt it gives to me.
Not that he regrets the farm,
but with nothing to resist him,
he misses the zest to fight.

You see a cruel act
but you'll play out your part
in dreams cut down, arranged for another's delight,
the dry whiff of long-pressed hopes.

The plants still live.
He knows they grip the earth tough and stubborn as weather
or himself.
You won't catch him
pushing up the mazes of their roots
or kicking destruction into their plucky stems.
Even this violence is a masque of harvest.
Dry your tears and remember.
Plant flowers, child,
plant flowers and tell this story.

HOLLYHOCKS

I

Fighting the tomatoes and sweet corn for light,
those wayward flowers clustered in my mother's garden.
Too stately for weeds, too plentiful
to be cherished, they spread in tight bunches,
nodding over the clothesline, peering in the kitchen.
They stuck close to the house, renewed each year
in the same places, safe from the plow,
safe from rooting hogs.
If their seeds wind-scattered beyond the hen house,
they tumbled upsprouted. Nothing lived easily
among the fireweed, the goldenrod
and the sharp rows of milo.

II

I stripped the showy spikes
and arranged my floral booty on the grass.
A toothpick jammed through the stem,
and each flower became a grand lady
draped in cloth of burgundy or scarlet.
Headless, flat-chested as I,
they glided in cotillions and quadrilles,
given grace by my hands.
But when I heard my father's tractor
and saw him driving up the pasture lane,
I left them motionless, dumb,

to run to the big wooden gate
and swing it open for him.
The discarded ladies lolled on the grass,
their flounces wrinkling into torn petals.

III
As he drove through the gate I held,
he looked straight ahead, and I swung behind him,
my greeting overcome by the machine's noise.
Mother's face pressed against the window, distorted
by the glass, and I knew just how she stood:
leaning forward, on one foot, hands braced on the sink.
The tractor sputtered out its hold on my father
and I watched his leg clear the seat
and touch him to the earth.
His face was caked with the gray soil he cultivated,
matching the evening drab of the farmyard,
the gravel, the silo and the elms indistinguishable
by color. With the strangling gray of dusk,
the hollyhocks were dull as pigweeds,
each bloom a faded trumpet, without sound.

PROGRESSION

You are the farmer's daughter,
corn-fed, apple-cheeked,
a local yokel from a jerkwater town
where tractors cruise the gut on Main Street
and Loretta keeps tabs from the five and dime.

You are the round little Swede,
snub-nosed, tongue-tied,
who rises at the crack of dawn
to milk the cows, slop the hogs
and cut across the corn to school.

You are the first to go to college,
one hundred homesick miles away,
straw behind ear, manure on shoes,

and a coke date after the Kansas game
where Husky the Corncob yelled in your face.

You marry the hayseed in ROTC blue,
decide graduate school's not for you,
pack Sunbeam skillets and Bake-King tin
to honeymoon at the Holiday Inn
where Tom and Sharon put cornflakes in the bed
and undutiful thoughts come into your head.

You are not the first to divorce.
"Grandma did and she was good!"
but Grandmother left that city slicker,
let him go straight to the dogs with corn liquor
and settled down with an old-country man.

Your lovers are men who never remember
if you're Iowa-born or Dakota-bred
but they've all hit I-80 on the way to Frisco,
sent corny postcards from Bosselman's Cafe:
"God, but I miss you. God, but it's flat."

You are the ugly American
in blue jeans, t-shirts and mirror shades.
The dollar's strong, your accent's stronger,
cracking gum, munching popcorn, peanut butter, chocolate bars –
"Why *can't* the Europeans take us like we are?"
You are home again, home again, wiser of course.
"Fine," you practice, like a salesman's spiel.
The same old cornfield east of the house,
Mom and Dad on the stoop, with the usual joke,
"Always glad to see you come – always glad to see you go."

Fredrick Zydek ℘

Frederick Zydek has published eight collections of poetry. His third, *Ending the Fast*, included a quartet entitled "Songs from the Quinault Valley," which won the Sarah Foley O'Loughlen Award; *T'KOPECHUCK: The Buckley Poems*, his ninth, is forthcoming from Winthrop Press. A new chapbook, *Hooked On Fish*, will be released from The Holmes House Chapbook Series later this year. Zydek's work has also appeared in *The Antioch Review*, *Cimmaron Review*, *Cricket*, *Danse Macabre*, *New England Review*, *Nimrod*, *Poetry*, *Prairie Schooner*, *Poetry Northwest*, *Yankee* and others. Zydek has more than 800 publishing credits which include personal essays, fiction, academic articles, plays, poems and reviews. This poem is published in *The Sandhills: II*.

℘

Nouns

Nouns have eyes of their own,
see to it things get named
and stay that way. They know
how to outwait the darkness,
slip, slight and painted
through the long silence.

Each is a cell pulling apart
at the seams. Some have long
liquid arms, others stand so short
they vanish the moment they're touched.
The best are smeared with questions,
enclose themselves
between short stemmed commas.

Some wrap themselves in shadows,

hoard the special names of spices.
Others come thin as whispers;
some, more plump than pudding,
drag their feet, wear mud
on their boots and close
their metaphors like traps.

A SANDHILLS BIBLIOGRAPHY

∽

1970s

Sanders, Mark. *First Hunt.* Ord, Nebraska: Sandhills Press, 1979.

1980s

Dwyer, David. *Other Men and Other Women.* The Plains Poetry Series, Vol. 4. Ord, Nebraska: Sandhills Press, 1988.

Lietz, Robert. *The Inheritance.* The Plains Poetry Series, Vol. 5. Ord, Nebraska: Sandhills Press, 1988.

Sanders, Mark. *Ghosts of a Christmas Past.* Ord, Nebraska: Sandhills Press, 1980.

Sanders, Mark and J.V. Brummels, eds. *On Common Ground: The Poetry of William Kloefkorn, Ted Kooser, Greg Kuzma, and Don Welch.* Ord, Nebraska: Sandhills Press, 1983.

Sanders, Mark, ed. *The Sandhills & Other Geographies: Poets of the Great Plains, I: An Anthology of Nebraska Poetry.* Ord, Nebraska: Sandhills Press, 1980.

Sanders, Mark, ed. *The Sandhills & Other Geographies: Poets of the Great Plains, II* Ord, Nebraska: Sandhills Press, 1981.

Scheele, Roy. *Pointing Out the Sky.* The Plains Poetry Series, Vol. 3. Ord, Nebraska: Sandhills Press, 1985.

Stillwell, Mary Kathryn. *Moving to Malibu.* The Plains Poetry Series, Vol. 6. Ord, Nebraska: Sandhills Press, 1988.

Sutter, Barton. *Pine Creek Parish Hall and Other Poems.* The Plains Poetry Series, Vol. 2. Ord, Nebraska: Sandhills Press, 1985.

West, Kathleene. *The Farmer's Daughter.* The Plains Poetry Series, Vol. 7. Ord, Nebraska: Sandhills Press, 1988.

West, Kathleene. *Plainswoman.* The Plains Poetry Series, Vol. 1. Ord, Nebraska: Sandhills Press, 1985.

1990s

Cherry, Kelly. *The Poem: An Essay.* Main-Travelled Roads #14. Grand Island, Nebraska and League City, Texas: Sandhills Press, 1999.

Dubrow, Heather. *Transformation and Repetition.* Main-Travelled Roads #12. Ord, Nebraska: Sandhills Press, 1997.

Holland, Larry. *My Link to the Plains.* Main-Travelled Roads #3.
Ord, Nebraska: Sandhills Press, 1996.

Kloefkorn, William. *Among the Living.* Main-Travelled Roads #17.
Grand Island, Nebraska and Pearland, Texas: Sandhills Press,
1999.

Kooser, Ted. *Riding with Colonel Carter: An Essay and Two Poems.* Main-
Travelled Roads #15. Grand Island, Nebraska and League City,
Texas: Sandhills Press, 1999.

McCleery, David. *Seven Poems.* Main-Travelled Roads #6. Ord,
Nebraska: Sandhills Press, 1996.

Reiter, Thomas. *Prairie of the Universe.* Main-Travelled Roads #7. Ord,
Nebraska: Sandhills Press, 1996.

Russell, CarolAnn. *Without Reservation: The Wannabe Poems.* Main-
Travelled Roads #4. Ord, Nebraska: Sandhills Press, 1996.

Sanders, Mark. *A Bibliographic Introduction to Poetry in Nebraska.*
MonoGraph #1. Ord, Nebraska: Sandhills Press, 1992.

Sanders, Mark. *Breaking Windows and Guns: Two Essays.* Main-Travelled
Roads #10. Ord, Nebraska: Sandhills Press, 1997.

Sanders, Mark. *Country Western.* Main-Travelled Roads #1. Ord,
Nebraska: Sandhills Press, 1996.

Sanders, Mark. *Plain Sense.* Ord, Nebraska: Sandhills Press, 1998.

Sanders, Mark, ed. *The Decade Dance: A Celebration of Poems.* Ord,
Nebraska: Sandhills Press, 1991.

Sanders, Mark, ed. *The Plains Sense of Things: Eight Poets from Outstate
Nebraska.* Grand Island, Nebraska and Texas City, Texas:
Sandhills Press, 1997.

Sanders, Mark, ed. *The Plains Sense of Things 2: Eight Poets from Lincoln,
Nebraska.* Grand Island, Nebraska and Texas City, Texas:
Sandhills Press, 1997.

Sanders, Mark, ed. *The Plains Sense of Things, 3: A Tribute to Larry Holland.*
Grand Island, Nebraska and Pearland, Texas: Sandhills Press,
1999.

Scheele, Roy. *Short Suite.* Main-Travelled Roads #11. Ord, Nebraska:
Sandhills Press, 1997.

Schmitz, Barbara. "How to Get Out of the Body." Grand Island,
Nebraska and Pearland, Texas: Sandhills Press, 1999.

Schmitz, Barbara. *How to Get Out of the Body.* The Plains Poetry Series
#9. Grand Island, Nebraska and Pearland, Texas: Sandhills
Press, 1999.

Schmitz, Barbara. *The Lives of the Saints*. Main-Travelled Roads #8. Ord, Nebraska: Sandhills Press, 1996.

Townsend, Ann, and David Baker. *Holding Katherine*. Main-Travelled Roads #5. Ord, Nebraska: Sandhills Press, 1996.

Wallace, Ronald. *Worry and Other Stories*. Main-Travelled Roads #2. Ord, Nebraska: Sandhills Press, 1996.

Welch, Don. *The Breeder of Archangels: A Requiem for Stanley Smith*. Main-Travelled Roads #18. Grand Island, Nebraska and Pearland, Texas: Sandhills Press, 1999.

Welch, Don. *The Marginalist and other poems*. The Plains Poetry Series Vol. 8. Ord, Nebraska: Sandhills Press, 1992.

Welch, Don. *Never Write in a Glass House*. Main-Travelled Roads #9. Ord, Nebraska: Sandhills Press, 1997.

West, Kathleene. *Death of a Regional Poet: Canto One*. Main-Travelled Roads #13. Texas City, Texas: Sandhills Press, 1998.

2000s

Aronson, Rebecca. *Creature, Creature*. Lewiston, ID: Main-Travelled Roads, 2007.

Benevento, Joe. *Some of My Best Friends and Other Fictions*. Lewiston, ID: Lewis-Clark Press, 2008.

Cherry, Kelly. *The Globe and the Brain: On Place in Fiction*. Lewiston, ID: Talking River Publications, 2006.

Coomer, Paula. *Devil at the Crossroads*. Lewiston, ID: Lewis-Clark Press, 2006.

Coomer, Paula. *Road*. Grand Island, Nebraska and Lewiston, Idaho: Sandhills Press, 2006.

Coomer, Paula. *Summer of Government Cheese*. Lewiston, ID: Lewis-Clark Press, 2007.

Diaconoff, Cara. *Unmarriageable Daughters: Stories*. Lewiston, ID: Lewis-Clark Press, 2008.

Evans, David Allen. *The Celebration: Three Stories*. Pearland, Texas and Grand Island, Nebraska: Sandhills Press, 2000.

Evans, Justin. *Four Way Stop*. Lewiston, Idaho: Sandhills Press, 2004.

Gotschall, Benjamin. *Where It Happened*. Scotia, Nebraska and Nacogdoches, Texas: Sandhills Press, 2008.

Holden, Jonathan. *Mama's Boys: A Double Life*. Lewiston, ID: Lewis-Clark Press, 2007.

Keen, Suzanne. *Milk Glass Mermaid*. Lewiston, ID: Lewis-Clark Press, 2007.

Kloefkorn, William. *Sunrise, Dayglow, Sunset, Moon*. Lewiston, ID: Talking River Publications, 2004.

Kolosov, Jacqueline, and Kirsten Sundberg Lunstrum. *The Sincerest Form of Flattery: Contemporary Women Writers on Forerunners in Fiction*. Lewiston, ID: Lewis-Clark Press, 2008.

Kolosov, Jacqueline. *Vago*. Lewiston, ID: Lewis-Clark Press, 2007.

Kosmicki, Greg. *For My Son in a Mud Room*. Grand Island, Nebraska and Pearland, Texas: Sandhills Press, 2000.

Kosmicki, Greg. *Tables, Chairs, Wall, Window*. Grand Island, Nebraska and Pearland, Texas: Sandhills Press, 2000.

Kosmicki, Greg. *We Have Always Been Coming to This Morning*. Lewiston, Idaho and Grand Island, Nebraska: Sandhills Press, 2007.

Kuzma, Greg. *A Day in the World*. Lewiston, ID: Lewis-Clark Press, 2009.

Kuzma, Greg. *For My Brother*. Lewiston, ID: Lewis-Clark Press, 2009.

Kuzma, Greg. *McKeever Bridge*. Grand Island, Nebraska: Sandhills Press, 2002.

Kvern, Julie. *A Conversation with Mary Clearman Blew*. Lewiston, ID: Talking River Publications, 2008.

Madigan, Kelly. *Born in the House of Love*. Lewiston, Idaho: Sandhills Press, 2005.

Mathes, Jerry D. *The Journal West*. Lewiston, ID: Lewis-Clark Press, 2009.

Mathes, Jerry D. *Twelve Lovers, Lost and Found*. Lewiston, ID: Talking River Publications, 2004.

Oatman, Judy K. *Rocks that Heal*. Lewiston, ID: Talking River Publications, 2006.

Oatman, Judy K. *Sunrise*. Lewiston, ID: Talking River Publications, 2007.

Oness, C. Mikal. *Oracle Bones*. Lewiston, ID: Lewis-Clark Press, 2007.

Pashley, Jennifer. *States*. Lewiston, ID: Lewis-Clark Press, 2007.

Sanders, Mark. *A Dissimulation of Birds*. Grand Island, Nebraska: Crane Editions, 2002.

Sanders, Mark. *Epistle to a Young Poet: Instructions for Life*. Grand Island, Nebraska: Sandhills Press, 2003.

Sanders, Mark. *The Rocking Horse Waltz*. Grand Island, Nebraska: Sandhills Press, 2003.

Schmitz, Barbara. *The Upside Down Heart*. Grand Island, Nebraska: Sandhills Press, 2002.

Smith, Judy R. *Yellowbird*. Lewiston, ID: Lewis-Clark Press, 2007.

Smith, R. T. *Ensemble*. Lewiston, ID: Talking River Publications, 2006.

Strauser, Judith. *The Reason/Unreason Project*. Lewiston, ID: Lewis-Clark Press, 2006.

Welch, Don. *Inklings: Poems Old and New*. Grand Island, Nebraska and Pearland, Texas: Sandhills Press, 2001.

Welch, Don. "Two Poems." Pearland, Texas: Sandhills Press, 2001.

Welch, Don. *The Yarn Bin*. Main-Travelled Roads #20. Grand Island, Nebraska and Pearland, Texas: Sandhills Press, 2001.

Welch, Don. *When Memory Gives Dust a Face*. Lewiston, ID: Lewis-Clark Press, 2008.

Broadsides

Barnes, Jim. "Crow White." 1998 Nebraska Literature Festival Keepsake Broadsides, Series 1, #G. Drawing by Mark Sanders. Ord, Nebraska: Sandhills Press, 1998.

Barnes, Jim. "The Poor Fox." 1998 Nebraska Literature Festival Keepsake Broadsides, Series 1, #H. Drawing by Mark Sanders. Ord, Nebraska: Sandhills Press, 1998.

Brummels, J.V. "Horsebreaker." 1998 Nebraska Literature Festival Keepsake Broadsides, Series 1, #I. Drawing by Mark Sanders. Ord, Nebraska: Sandhills Press, 1998.

Brummels, J.V. "Possum." 1998 Nebraska Literature Festival Keepsake Broadsides, Series 1, #Y. Drawing by Mark Sanders. Ord, Nebraska: Sandhills Press, 1998.

Brummels, J.V. "Wildlife." 1998 Nebraska Literature Festival Keepsake Broadsides, Series 1, #Z. Drawing by Mark Sanders. Ord, Nebraska: Sandhills Press, 1998.

Evans, David Allen. "Ford Pickup." 1998 Nebraska Literature Festival Keepsake Broadsides, Series 1, #Q. Drawing by Mark Sanders. Ord, Nebraska: Sandhills Press, 1998.

Evans, David Allen. "Next Morning." 1998 Nebraska Literature Festival Keepsake Broadsides, Series 1, #R. Drawing by Mark Sanders. Ord, Nebraska: Sandhills Press, 1998.

Fort, Charles. "Ode to Those Not Born in Nebraska." Broadside. Ord, Nebraska: Sandhilles Press, 2001.

Hansen, Twyla. "Blue Herons." 1998 Nebraska Literature Festival Keepsake Broadsides, Series 1, #S. Drawing by Mark Sanders. Ord, Nebraska: Sandhills Press, 1998.

Hansen, Twyla. "Milk." 1998 Nebraska Literature Festival Keepsake Broadsides, Series 2, #II. Drawing by Mark Sanders. Ord,

Nebraska: Sandhills Press, 1998.

Harrison, Neil. "Prayer and Omen." 1998 Nebraska Literature Festival Keepsake Broadsides, Series 1, #W. Drawing by Mark Sanders. Ord, Nebraska: Sandhills Press, 1998.

Hoffman, Joan. "Epiphany." 1998 Nebraska Literature Festival Keepsake Broadsides, Series 1, #D. Drawing by Mark Sanders. Ord, Nebraska: Sandhills Press, 1998.

Holland, Larry. "Destiny." 1998 Nebraska Literature Festival Keepsake Broadsides, Series 2, #IV. Drawing by Mark Sanders. Ord, Nebraska: Sandhills Press, 1998.

Holland, Larry. "'The Eye Altering Alters All.'" 1998 Nebraska Literature Festival Keepsake Broadsides, Series 2, #III. Drawing by Mark Sanders. Ord, Nebraska: Sandhills Press, 1998.

Holland, Larry. "Walk on Water." 1998 Nebraska Literature Festival Keepsake Broadsides, Series 1, #J. Drawing by Mark Sanders. Ord, Nebraska: Sandhills Press, 1998.

Holm, Bill. "Without TV." 1998 Nebraska Literature Festival Keepsake Broadsides, Series 1, #V. Drawing by Mark Sanders. Ord, Nebraska: Sandhills Press, 1998.

Kloefkorn, William. "Brothers." 1998 Nebraska Literature Festival Keepsake Broadsides, Series 1, #A. Drawing by Mark Sanders. Ord, Nebraska: Sandhills Press, 1998.

Kloefkorn, William. "from 'loony.'" 1998 Nebraska Literature Festival Keepsake Broadsides, Series 2, #IX. Drawing by Mark Sanders. Ord, Nebraska: Sandhills Press, 1998.

Kloefkorn, William. "from 'loony.'" 1998 Nebraska Literature Festival Keepsake Broadsides, Series 2, #X. Drawing by Mark Sanders. Ord, Nebraska: Sandhills Press, 1998.

Kooser, Ted. "Beer Bottle." 1998 Nebraska Literature Festival Keepsake Broadsides, Series 2, #VIII. Drawing by Mark Sanders. Ord, Nebraska: Sandhills Press, 1998.

Kooser, Ted. "Laundry." 1998 Nebraska Literature Festival Keepsake Broadsides, Series 1, #T. Drawing by Mark Sanders. Ord, Nebraska: Sandhills Press, 1998.

Kooser, Ted. "Snow Fence." 1998 Nebraska Literature Festival Keepsake Broadsides, Series 2, #VII. Drawing by Mark Sanders. Ord, Nebraska: Sandhills Press, 1998.

Lee, David. "Summer Solstice." 1998 Nebraska Literature Festival Keepsake Broadsides, Series 1, #O. Drawing by Mark Sanders. Ord, Nebraska: Sandhills Press, 1998.

Lee, David. "Song E. U. Washburn Heard While Tending Roses Over the Grave of Philemon and Baucis Rojas." Keepsake Broadside. Drawing by Mark Sanders. Ord, Nebraska: Sandhills Press, 1998.

McCleery, Nancy. "Girl Talk (Bosh/Save)." 1998 Nebraska Literature Festival Keepsake Broadsides, Series 1, #P. Drawing by Mark Sanders. Ord, Nebraska: Sandhills Press, 1998.

Russell, CarolAnn. "Wings." 1998 Nebraska Literature Festival Keepsake Broadsides, Series 1, #C. Drawing by Mark Sanders. Ord, Nebraska: Sandhills Press, 1998.

Sanders, Mark. "The Creighton Pool Hall." 1998 Nebraska Literature Festival Keepsake Broadsides, Series 2, #V. Drawing by Mark Sanders. Ord, Nebraska: Sandhills Press, 1998.

Sanders, Mark. "Elms." 1998 Nebraska Literature Festival Keepsake Broadides, Series 1,#M. Drawing by Mark Sanders. Ord, Nebraska: Sandhills Press, 1998.

Sanders, Mark. "No Accounts, 1948." 1998 Nebraska Literature Festival Keepsake Broadsides, Series 1, #K. Drawing by Mark Sanders. Ord, Nebraska: Sandhills Press, 1998.

Sanders, Mark. "The Significant Otter." 1998 Nebraska Literature Festval Keepsake Broadsides, Series 1, #L. Drawing by Mark Sanders. Ord, Nebraska: Sandhills Press, 1998.

Sanders, Mark. "The World." 1998 Nebraska Literature Festival Keepsake Broadsides, Series 2, #VI. Drawing by Mark Sanders. Ord, Nebraska: Sandhills Press, 1998.

Sanders, Mark. "Hands." Keepsake Broadside. Drawing by Mark Sanders. Ord, Nebraska: Sandhills Press, 1998.

Sanders, Mark. "On Horseback, Hell's Gate Canyon, October." Center for Arts and History Reading. Lewiston, Idaho: Sandhills Press, 2004.

Scheele, Roy. "The Cuckoo." 1998 Nebraska Literature Festival Keepsake Broadsides, Series 1, #U. Drawing by Mark Sanders. Ord, Nebraska: Sandhills Press, 1998.

Schmitz, Barbara. "Supper." 1998 Nebraska Literature Festival Keepsake Broadsides, Series 1, #I. Drawing by Mark Sanders. Ord, Nebraska: Sandhills Press, 1998.

Verhines-Sanders, Kimberly. "Dry Spell." 1998 Nebraska Literature Festival Keepsake Broadsides, Series 2, #XIII. Drawing by Mark Sanders. Ord, Nebraska: Sandhills Press, 1998.

Welch, Don. "Baltimore Oriole." 1998 Nebraska Literature Festival Keepsake Broadsides, Series 1, #XII. Drawing by Mark

Sanders. Ord, Nebraska: Sandhills Press, 1998.

Welch, Don. "Carved by Obadiah Verity." 1998 Nebraska Literature Festival Keepsake Broadsides, Series 2, #XI. Drawing by Mark Sanders. Ord, Nebraska: Sandhills Press, 1998.

Welch, Don. "Funeral at Ansley." 1998 Nebraska Literature Festival Keepsake Broadsides, Series 1, #E. Drawing by Mark Sanders. Ord, Nebraska: Sandhills Press, 1998.

Welch, Don. "Nebraska." 1998 Nebraska Literature Festival Keepsake Broadsides, Series 1, #F. Drawing by Mark Sanders. Ord, Nebraska: Sandhills Press, 1998.

Welch, Don. "Two Poems." Keepsake Broadside. Pearland, Texas: Sandhills Press, 2001

Welch, Don. "The Chicken Poem." Keepsake Broadside. Drawing by Mark Sanders. Ord, Nebraska: Sandhills Press, 1999.

Welch, Don. "The Hawk." Keepsake Broadside. Drawing by Mark Sanders. Ord, Nebraska: Sandhills Press, 1998.

West, Kathleene. "The Loneliness of the Long-Distance Lover." 1998 Nebraska Literature Festival Keepsake Broadsides, Series 1, #B. Drawing by Mark Sanders. Ord, Nebraska: Sandhills Press, 1998.

West, Kathleene. "Pastoral." 1998 Nebraska Literature Festival Keepsake Broadsides, Series 1, #N. Drawing by Mark Sanders. Ord, Nebraska: Sandhills Press, 1998.

Zarzyski, Paul. "Antipasto!" 1998 Nebraska Literature Festival Keepsake Broadsides, Series 1, #X. Drawing by Mark Sanders. Ord, Nebraska: Sandhills Press, 1998.